How to
Brilliant

Prentice Hall LIFE

If life is what you make it, then making it better starts here.

What we learn today can change our lives tomorrow. It can change our goals or change our minds; open up new opportunities or simply inspire us to make a difference. That's why we have created a new breed of books that do more to help you make more of *your* life.

Whether you want more confidence or less stress, a new skill or a different perspective, we've designed *Prentice Hall Life* books to help you to make a change for the better. Together with our authors we share a commitment to bring you the brightest ideas and best ways to manage your life, work and wealth.

In these pages we hope you'll find the ideas you need for the life *you* want. Go on, help yourself.

It's what you make it

* * *

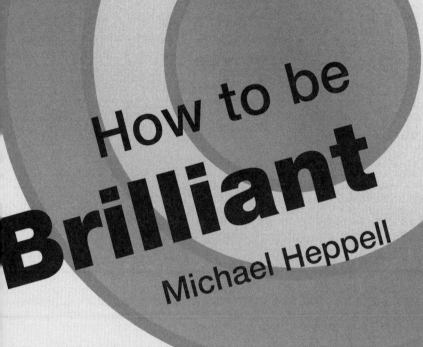

How to be Brilliant

Michael Heppell

2nd edition

change your ways in 90 days!

PEARSON

Prentice Hall

LIFE

Harlow, England • London • New York • Boston • San Francisco • Toronto • Sydney • Singapore • Hong Kong
Tokyo • Seoul • Taipei • New Delhi • Cape Town • Madrid • Mexico City • Amsterdam • Munich • Paris • Milan

PEARSON EDUCATION LIMITED

Edinburgh Gate
Harlow CM20 2JE
Tel: +44 (0)1279 623623
Fax: +44 (0)1279 431059

First published in 2004
Second edition published in Great Britain in 2007

© Pearson Education Limited 2004, 2007

ISBN: 978-0-273-71451-4

British Library Cataloguing in Publication Data
A CIP catalogue record for this book can be obtained from the British Library

10 9 8 7 6 5 4 3 2 1
11 10 09 08 07

Typeset in Photina MT 10pt by 3
Printed and bound in Great Britain by Ashford Colour Press, Hampshire

The Publishers' policy is to use paper manufactured from sustainable forests.

For finding brilliance in everything,

I dedicate this book to the love of my life Christine

and to our children Michael and Sarah

Contents

About The Author

Michael Heppell works with thousands of people every year presenting at conferences, training staff and arranging 'How to Be Brilliant' seminars. Well known for his unique style, Michael has the ability to translate complex models into easy-to-use tools that anyone can apply for rapid success.

He works with a wide range of individuals and organizations around the world ranging from entrepreneurs to Premiership footballers, in PLCs and prisons. In fact anywhere where there is the desire to be brilliant!

Michael is also the author of *Five Star Service, One Star Budget* and has recorded several audio programmes including the world's first exam success audio download programme.

He lives in Northumberland, England with his wife Christine and their two children.

So why a revised edition?

When I wrote *How to be Brilliant* I would have been thrilled if anyone other than my Mum had bought it. Now *How to be Brilliant* is heading towards its fourth birthday and I have been stunned at the results. It has been translated into 14 different languages, it's available in bookshops in more than 70 countries around the world and has had multiple reprints. So why change a winning formula?

Well, as you'll read, part of the ethos of *How to be Brilliant* is to keep on moving to the next level and, I thought, it could be even better. The first major change is the focus. The original book was written for a business audience, it was listed in the business sections and spent two and a half years as a top ten business book. But business isn't the main reason why people were reading it. People want to know how to be brilliant in all areas of their life, so that's what this book does now – it will work as a guide to help you to be brilliant in any area of your life. And you'll do it brilliantly.

There are also 3 new chapters: to inspire you to take action; to help get you beyond brilliant and to show you how to overcome obstacles.

Finally, I've given the manuscript a facelift, chopped out some of the good bits (that will make sense to you later) and added an exercise checklist to help keep you on track.

Preface

Have you ever had a moment in your life when you made a decision, and your destiny changed in a second? Exciting isn't it how those small moments impact upon the rest of your life. As you read, take a moment to think about the moments that changed your life. Ask yourself if you were controlling these changes or were they controlling you? Did they improve your life in the short term or was it longer before you saw the benefits (or are you still waiting)?

I want to begin by telling you about some of the brilliant moments that changed my life. I discovered as I sat down to list them that there were dozens, but some had a bigger impact than others towards creating *How to be Brilliant*. I'll share them with you.

I left school aged 16 and immediately started to work in my father's business as an apprentice roofer. I realized after about a week that it wasn't for me and I made a decision to leave. Seven years later I built up the courage to actually tell my Dad that I was never destined to be in a conventional business and I had found a new job. He was thrilled for me! I discovered that no matter what, he wanted me to be happy.

Brill Bit

Never do a job you don't love. You spend a third of your life at work – make it a pleasure! If you don't love it, don't do it!

My father taught me a huge amount about values. He would never take an easier route to make a quick profit, he would commit to spending hours with apprentices to teach them the highest quality craftsmanship and give unconditionally of his time and resources to ensure something was right. He trained the British roofing team, who went on to win the world championships (I bet you never knew there was a roofing world championship!) and helped hundreds of people around the world. This was my first experience of brilliance.

I got involved with working with young people first as a volunteer, then as a professional youth worker. Next I managed a large project with lots of different charities at the National Garden Festival in Gateshead. I had the job of ensuring the charities had everything they needed to be successful. It wasn't long before I realized some charities were going to raise a lot more than others. In fact, looking at the figures each week, I noticed that 20 per cent of the charities were raising 80 per cent of the money and the other 80 per cent were fighting over the remaining 20 per cent. One organization in particular stood out: the Northumberland Wildlife Trust. They seemed to do everything better than most, but on closer inspection I discovered the key to their success and it has remained with me for life: their team was brilliant! They arrived early, left late, worked harder and connected with more people than any other organization. Did they raise more money? You bet they did! Day after day, week after week. I was puzzled, why didn't others spot what they were doing and re-model their strategies accordingly? It's only now that I truly understand why.

Brill Bit

Brilliance does not happen by accident. It is all about the planning, the work and the skills.

I eventually became a fundraiser myself for a charity that became the most successful ever in the North of England. Looking back, I know that some of the techniques I was applying were great personal development tools. The only way we could be so successful was by having a great attitude, by being able to set new standards, by breaking out of limiting beliefs that would hold many other people back.

My next job was working with another charity but this time I was responsible for bringing in large donations. One day I had the privilege of meeting with a man called David Brown. He's the man who invented the Caterpillar, the large, split-axle truck that we see in quarries throughout the world. David Brown was a very gentle man but completely focused. After a long conversation with him (with me asking most of the questions about his life, and what he had achieved), he turned to me and said, 'Michael, what are you doing about your own personal development?' I didn't really understand the question, but after some soul searching, I knew the time had come for me to take some positive action.

I started to read books. The first one was called *Think and Grow Rich* by Napoleon Hill. I have since read that book over ten times. The next book was *How to Win Friends and Influence People* by Dale Carnegie. Two classics. I realized that if I wanted to improve myself (and others) I had to get additional knowledge. To get that information I devoted myself to consistent and never ending improvement. I made a commitment to read a book a week and did so for two years. That is one of the reasons why I thank you for reading this book because reading can be hard. Why not set a personal challenge to make this the fastest book you have ever read?

When I was reading a book a week, I was also listening to as many tapes from as many different authors and experts as I could. I booked myself on to personal development courses because I realized that if I wanted to improve, I had to invest in my own future. Much of this book is influenced by many of those early books I read and tapes I listened to.

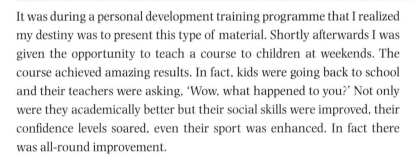

Brill Bit

Read, read and read! Become a glutton for knowledge. You can learn a person's life's work from one book. When applied, every penny and every second you invest in your learning will pay back at a rate you could only have dreamed of.

It was during a personal development training programme that I realized my destiny was to present this type of material. Shortly afterwards I was given the opportunity to teach a course to children at weekends. The course achieved amazing results. In fact, kids were going back to school and their teachers were asking, 'Wow, what happened to you?' Not only were they academically better but their social skills were improved, their confidence levels soared, even their sport was enhanced. In fact there was all-round improvement.

Teachers started to come to see our courses and began to understand what we were doing. It wasn't long before there was a lot of interest from educational bodies. I was given the opportunity to teach teachers some of the skills and techniques that we were applying in our programme.

The day I walked through the school gates to teach teachers for the first time was the day I realized that teaching teachers is tough! It may surprise you. I stood up in front of a group of teachers and was explaining passionately many different ideas and how they could possibly work in their particular school.

The teachers were not engaged at all. I asked myself, 'What's wrong with these people, why don't they understand – why is it that they won't take these ideas and use them right now?'

I made a great mistake when I used a so-called classic method to take control of the situation and asked, 'Does anyone have any questions or comments?' Can you imagine my surprise when about fifty hands shot up! I panicked and tried to pick someone whom I thought looked old and 'weak'. Big mistake, old people are not weak!

She asked,

'Whose research is this based on?'

'Where are the scientific facts to back up your ideas?'

'What's the cognitive process in the neo-cortex when the brain processes positive language?'

To be honest she'd lost me after, 'What's the . . .' Have you ever had that sick feeling in your stomach at the time you think it will never go away? For the rest of the day these teachers gave me the hardest training experience of my life.

I realized it was all very well knowing that these ideas worked, but how was I going to get the supporting scientific evidence?

Right person right time

Do you believe the right people appear at the right time in your life? I do. With a head full of questions, I met a great man called Professor John MacBeath OBE. At that time he was Head of Quality in Education at the University of Strathclyde, Glasgow. He moved on to be Professor of Leadership in the Faculty of Education at Cambridge University. Here's a man who really knows his stuff, and he offered to help with our work in education. We have become very close friends because he was able to demonstrate not only how the ideas worked, but *why* they worked. Once we added to this the research to back up the ideas, we had a winning combination. I was so excited. Once again I was in a learning curve, a huge accelerated learning curve! This time we could touch the lives of many millions of young people through working in education.

Brill Bit

The right people turn up at the right time – so keep your eyes open. You never know, the person sitting opposite you on the train, or that friend of a friend could hold the answer to so many questions in your life. But if you don't talk to them, you'll never know.

Within the space of a few months, we moved from school halls to The World Thinking Conference in Singapore, and had the privilege of presenting our work to an international audience of people from 52 countries. We were able to demonstrate different ideas and techniques which were really working in education. Our model is now used in many countries throughout the world, and I am very proud to have been a part of it. I also realized in Singapore it was time to do something for *me* . . .

Ninety days later I'd resigned from my job, moved house, written a new series of training sessions, reset all my personal goals and started my own organization, Michael Heppell Limited, with a vision to positively influence one million lives.

Introduction

Fed up with poor results? Thought so.

If you're tired of putting in hours of effort for measly rewards or if you're fed up with doing the same thing week in week out, you need to know the secret of brilliance. Every year a so-called 'lucky few' receive recognition, rewards and success way beyond their wildest imagination. They go on to positively influence those around them and make a genuine difference. Others look on and comment on how fortunate they are with their lucky breaks. Well the truth is far from that. The secret is they decided to be brilliant.

How to be Brilliant will give you the tools to find out exactly where you are now. Then to understand where it is you want to get to and develop strategies and powerful methods to get you there:

- as quickly as possible
- as economically as possible
- with as much fun as possible

You'll change your ways in 90 days.

You'll discover the specific characteristics of brilliant people so that you can learn and model from the best. Through many examples and personal stories, you'll discover how to use techniques to overcome the barriers that hold you back. You'll learn how to set a clear vision for an outstanding, brilliant future, and how to communicate with your friends, colleagues and family at a higher level.

With this foundation you'll create a vision and have an exciting 90-day plan to achieve your short-term goals. Then with a range of tried and tested tools and with new levels of energy and enthusiasm, you can move forward to create and achieve longer-term goals. You'll learn how to be proactive when faced with challenges and have over 50 tools at your disposal to move you to the level where you deserve to be.

Also in this revised edition you'll learn how those who are already brilliant work hard to be even better. Brilliance is a standard, not a skill. You'll be able to take the techniques learned for one area of your life and apply the same standards in other areas with minor adjustments – once you know the secrets to being brilliant.

The book is designed to be easy to use and is broken down into sections ensuring you learn at your own pace. 'Brill Bits' are designed to pull out key pieces of insight, learning or things you may want to look at more closely. So make a commitment now, and enjoy reading *How to be Brilliant*.

Getting the most from this book

This book can really change your life. But to do so, you need to *participate fully*. If I suggest to you that you should complete a task, then please do just that. Just sitting there reading this information isn't going to be enough. One of the things I know about my own personal life is that understanding something on an intellectual level is worthless. Life is about taking actions. It's about doing something. That's what's going to make the difference. The actions that you take now are going to affect your life massively in the future. Just acknowledging information is not enough.

Brill Bit

The secret is not in the knowing, it's in the doing.

Let me tell you what we're going to cover in this book.

First of all we want to look at getting a brilliant life balance. You'll do an exercise called 'The Wheel of Life'. The Wheel of Life isn't something that you're only going to do once. In fact, this whole programme isn't something you're only going to do once. This is something that I would like you to do on a regular basis. Why? Every time you visit your Wheel of Life you'll understand how your own personal development is improving. If you spot areas that you're starting to fall back on a little, you can immediately address those issues and step up.

We're going to look at the characteristics of brilliant people. What is it that makes a person brilliant? Do you think they are born brilliant? Or do you think they have characteristics that they put in place, certain things that they learn, and certain things that they strive for that make them brilliant? There are five key characteristics of brilliant people. If you apply those characteristics to your life, you are certain to move up to the next level. I'll guarantee you move closer towards brilliance.

Then we'll do some goal-setting. You need a strong 'Why' to move forward and engage in the tools – and techniques and goals are the best drivers.

You won't learn a system for goal-setting which is like the majority of others, because in my experience, the majority of goal-setting doesn't work. You'll not see any SMART* goals here!

Then we're going to look at the level at which you currently live your life. Are you doing a poor job? Are you doing a good job? Are you doing a fantastic job? Or are you doing a brilliant job? The people who are doing a consistently brilliant job seem to get the best results by far. In this book you'll discover how to get brilliant results every time. One of the things that stop you from getting brilliant results right now is probably your belief system. It's not for me to say whether your belief system is right or wrong. However, I know through experience, working with thousands and thousands of people, that it's our belief system that holds us back more than anything else. You created that belief system. We're going to explore what it is that you believe and why you believe it.

Wouldn't it be great if you could change your belief system right now and make it more empowering; a belief system designed by you, exclusively for you, that helps you step up and engage your life at an altogether different level? We'll explore this later in the book.

We're going to study Circles of Influence versus Circles of Concern. We all have many concerns in our lives, but the way to move on is to look at what we can influence, what we can change, the actions we can take rather than dwelling on our concerns and things we can't alter. You are going to put together a strategy, using a model that will move you forward very quickly. In fact, at a pace that will surprise you. When you

---

*SMART goals, meaning Specific Measurable Achievable Realistic with Timescale, have been taught by trainers, usually corporate, for years now. I have yet to meet a person who is currently living their life's vision through using the SMART system.

read this book again as a reminder in a month, two months, or a year's time, you'll look back and think, 'Wow, look how much I've changed!' The reason why you will have changed, and changed for the positive, is that you'll have worked on areas that you can personally influence in your life.

Towards the end of the book, we're going to explore your values system. Why spend time on values? Isn't that just something that develops through time? No. Values are something that we create. We create values in the same way we create a belief system, and then we create the evidence and the rules that support a belief system and that support our value system. So we're going to look in depth at our values, and understand how we created them in the first place.

You'll understand how the decisions you make every moment of every day make you the person you are. You'll make decisions about your current values that may change your life for ever. You might be lucky. You could read this chapter and say, 'That's me, right now, perfect values, perfect rules, I'm perfect!' Or maybe you'll be like 95 per cent of the population and say, 'Hold on a moment, they're not the right values, they're not the values that are going to get me to where I really need to be in my life.' You need brilliant values if you want to be brilliant in life.

And why do this on your own? The 'Brilliant teams' chapter will give you a range of techniques to help you work with others, get people on your side and save time. Blended with some cracking ideas for building rapport with others, this section is a must for anyone who deals with other human beings – and that's all of us!

Then we'll step up and set some big goals – stretch goals that at first may seem impossible – but with the application of the ideas contained on these pages, you'll soon see outstanding results.

You'll discover how to use an amazing visualization technique called Mental Rehearsal. Mental Rehearsal is used by top athletes. Brilliant performance doesn't happen by accident: it happens for a reason. Mental Rehearsal will show you how you can create the outcomes that you want on a consistent basis.

They are based on the techniques and systems of the very best people on the planet; the people who really know how to get results in an exciting and passionate way. I want to show you how you can set goals that really excite you, encourage you to take action and get the results that you desire.

At the end of the book, you put your brilliance into action and create enough personal leverage to make things happen.

In this revised edition you will also read how to go to the next level once you become brilliant, how to overcome obstacles that may hold you back and you can read a selection of success stories from people who, just like you, made a decision to read this book.

True and false will

When you make any decision you will do it with either true will or false will; let me explain the difference. False will is the most common. It's when people say they definitely will do something. Easy to say... True will means you will do it no matter what happens. I have been coached for the last two years by an incredible mentor called Peter Field. For the first year Peter seemed to focus entirely on how to build my 'true will' muscle. It works. Once this metaphoric muscle is strong it becomes much easier to take on new commitments, to know that you will see things through and your confidence soars.

My challenge to you is to use *How to be Brilliant* to build your true will muscle too.

Finally, I want to set up a little contract with you before we start properly.

Take a moment and give yourself a very honest mark out of 10 for how happy you are to learn new information. 10 is high, 0 is low.

Then give yourself a mark out of 10 for how happy you are to change. How do you feel about change? Is change something that you absolutely relish, that you love? Are you happy to try any new idea? When they say 'There's going to be a change programme', at work, if you're the one shouting, 'Yes, I love that' then give yourself a high mark. If you're not as happy about change, or if you don't want to change the way that you do things, give yourself a low mark. Again, 10 is high, 0 is low.

Then take those two numbers and multiply them together. You'll have a number somewhere between 0 and 100.

If you have 100 at this point, congratulations, there's no doubt that you'll get maximum value out of this book. If you are a 90, great, once again you can expect wonderful results. Between 80 and 90, you're doing well. Now as we start to get lower, I'll make a prediction. I bet the area that lets you down is your willingness to change. That's not true in all cases. However, people generally dislike change.

Brill Bit

Understanding the ideas in the book is fine. Your ability to put those ideas into action is what makes the big difference. So test yourself. Go for it!

90 days of Massive Action

So let's introduce the concept of a 90-day plan. The 90-day plan contains the actions you *must* take, not that you *should* take. In 90 days you can make huge shifts in your life and make a significant difference to your circumstances. Check today's date. Count forward 90 days and mentally mark your first 90 days.

90 days is great timeframe as it's long enough to change any personal habit, most circumstances and every belief. But short enough to remain excited about. You truly can change your ways in 90 days. You'll hear a lot about 90 days in this book.

Finally, please, please, please, please – I'm on my knees hands clasped here – do not think this is a one-off exercise. If I were to suggest that all you have to do to be fit is to go to the gym once, would you believe me? Wouldn't that be wonderful? Dream on! If you want to be physically fit, if you want to stay fit, you have to exercise on a regular basis. It's exactly the same with exercising your own personal development. You must work continuously. Every day, every week, every month, make sure you are immersing yourself with information.

Brill Bit

This is a programme for life. Just like being physically fit, being mentally fit requires constant work. But it's worth it!

With this in mind – take action now. Decide it's time to step up. Make a commitment right here right now to play full out. Make a commitment right here right now to improve your life, to step up to the next level and learn How to be Brilliant.

a

brilliant
life balance

We'll **begin with one** of the simplest but most effective ideas of personal development, the Wheel of Life. This is a way you can measure your own personal development. From the moment you wake up in the morning to the moment you go to bed, you're on a journey. And that journey needs to be mapped to ensure you're heading in the right direction. The Wheel of Life is a method for measuring each different key part of your life and your lifestyle to see that you're on the right path. On the opposite page you'll see a blank Wheel of Life. You're going to give yourself a mark on each one of the spokes when I describe each section of the Wheel of Life. You have to be honest. It's going to be a mark somewhere between 0 and 10. 0 will be right in the centre of the wheel. 10s are on the outside. The more honest you are with this process, the more you can chart your own personal growth. You can imagine how things are in the future and how you want them – this will help massively when we get into the Goal Setting chapters later in the book.

Brill Bit

This is PERSONAL development. The more honest you are with yourself, the better the results. To move forward effectively we have to recognize honestly where we are right now.

Now take your Wheel of Life, read the description of each section and then give yourself a mark.

Health

Are you the type of person who gets up in the morning and shouts, 'Yes. It's Monday morning, I've got so much energy'? You then leap out of bed, dive down the stairs, get your running kit on and run two or three miles to get the day started. On your return you have a nice shower. You are feeling great, and as you come downstairs everybody's looking at you and thinking, 'Yes, you're the picture of health.' When you see yourself in a mirror, you just can't help thinking 'I'm looking good'. You get into work or you go to school and people are saying to you 'Wow! I just don't believe how healthy you look.' You are just so vibrant. Everybody else around you could be catching the flu, they could be getting all sorts of

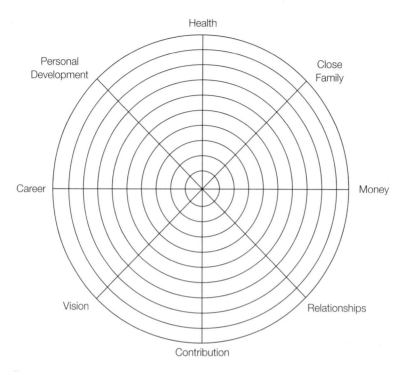

illness – dropping like flies. But not you, you are the one who is immune to all disease!

If that is truly you, if you're that type of person who really plays full out, gets to the end of the day and still has loads of energy, congratulations, you are a 10!

Or, perhaps you are the type of person who, when you are woken by the alarm clock – just as you hear the 'beep beep beep . . .' the first thing you do is you hit the snooze button for 9 more minutes of slumber bliss. It starts again, 'beep beep beep . . .' You hit snooze again, another 9 minutes, heaven. But 9 minutes later the damn thing goes off again, 'beep beep beep'. This time you think, 'If I get ready really really quickly, maybe skip breakfast, then I can have 9 more minutes!' It's a plan, so you click snooze one more time. It only feels like seconds then it goes off again. This time your irrational, exhausted mind is thinking, 'If I don't have a shower . . .' You eventually get out of bed to get ready.

As you walk past the mirror, you have a look and think, 'Oh my goodness; look at the state of that'. Faces smirk at the mess as you walk into the kitchen. You get to work or school. You feel a little bit of a sniffle coming on. Immediately you know what that means. 'It's that flu bug that's going round. I'm going to be ill tomorrow.' The next morning you wake up, it's snot city and you knew you were right!

For the rest of the week you just drag yourself through. You get home, absolutely trashed. You lie down on the sofa where your idea of relaxation equals watching TV. If that is you, the bad news is you are probably around a 2 or a 3. Most people will be somewhere in between. The good news is you are not a 1 – those people are too sick to read – so you're going to be a little bit higher up than that. Nevertheless, give yourself a very honest mark somewhere between 0 and 10 for how you feel about your health.

Close family

What sort of a relationship do you have with your closest family? There are lots of different ways we can measure that, but let me give you a couple of examples. Do you have the type of relationship where everybody is just really caring for each other? Everyone is really concerned about each other's needs and making sure things are just right for them?

Do you remember the old TV programme, *The Waltons*? Those guys lived on a mountain in a big white house and everything appeared to be perfect. Who could forget? 'Goodnight John boy, good night Mama!' *The Waltons* is guaranteed vomit-inducing TV these days, but to have that type of relationship, where you can live with people and have total respect for who they are, where they want to be, to give each other the freedom to move, to grow, to give true unconditional support, then that's a real close family relationship.

Or do you have the type of relationship where you think, 'Christmas is coming soon, sod the lot of them. They are getting nothing this year. And as for my brother, well he was supposed to ring me and he didn't, so I'm not ringing him. Yes, I know it's been ages since I called in to see my Mum, but you know it's the same distance both ways. I know she's 96, but there *is* a bus'?

If your relationship with your close family isn't what you think it should be; if you have kids and are not communicating with them in the right way; if your 'significant other' isn't making you feel significant or vice versa, then I want you to give yourself a really honest mark. You might be lucky; you might be high up. Or maybe you are not so fortunate and you know there are some challenges. The good news is, we are going to tackle those challenges in this book, so give yourself a mark for your 'Close Family' now.

Money

Yes – the dosh, cash, spendies, the readies. First the good news. It's not about how much money you have; it's about your relationship with money. You might be the type of person who, no matter how much you earn, you still have too much month at the end of the money! (I've met many people who suffer from this.) Your idea of a strategy for finances is to apply for a Visa card, and use it to pay off your Mastercard, and then you are going to get a new MBNA card to pay off your Visa card, and then you are going to get some store cards so you don't have to spend your money for a few months. Then the whole thing is going to build and build and build, and you are going to have a look at how many payments you've got to pay each month rather than how much money you're going to save. Then it's time to call a finance company to consolidate it into 'one easy payment' before starting all over again.

That type of financial management does not get you high marks on the Money spoke of your Wheel of Life.

Think very carefully about your finances. Perhaps you're the type of person who knows exactly where your money is going each month. You have a financial strategy in place. You have an understanding of how money works. You know that if you do ever need to borrow money, that you will have a strategy for paying it back which is completely within your means. You understand at any time where you are financially. But most importantly, you feel comfortable about money. Your relationship with money means that you understand it's always going to come in, it's always going to go out. That type of thinking and action gets higher marks.

Whichever way you look at it, be very honest with marking this area of life.

I agree **money isn't** the most important thing in life. However, **many of the most important** things in life are often **made easier** by your management of money.

Relationships

What type of friend are you? What type of work colleague are you? Think about the people whom you are closest to on a daily basis, and think about how they treat you. Imagine you are walking along the corridor and you see a group of people having a chat. They suddenly catch you out of the corner of their eye and they say, 'Oh oh, they're here, shhh they're here!' You walk up to them and say, 'What's going on?' and you know they were talking about something which they don't want you to hear. Immediately your mind starts to play all sorts of tricks. 'Were they talking about me?' 'Were they organizing an event that I'm not invited to?' Well, there might be a reason for that. Is it because you are the type of person whose idea of strictest confidence is only telling people one at a time? If you're the type of person who thinks well, you know, I've got to get myself absolutely sorted out first, and other people well, sod them, they can catch up later, I'm afraid you get a lower mark with this part of your Wheel of Life.

Or are you the type of person who really is a superb friend? The type of person who when friends or colleagues have a challenge or a problem they come to you, not just for sympathy, not just because you are going to be a shoulder to cry on, but because you give great advice? You have an absolute understanding. You have a level of care and passion that attracts people to come to you to be understood. Well if you are that type of person, it's great news because you get a higher mark here for your relationships. So give yourself a mark for Relationships on your Wheel of Life.

Contribution

If 'the secret of living is giving', then how would you measure your contribution? I'm not necessarily referring to financial contribution to worthy causes (although you may want to measure your contribution in that way). Contribution is about giving of your time, resources, energy and spirit without expectation of anything in return.

Are you thinking of ways to make your society better or complaining that things aren't what they used to be? Do you give first without any expectation of what may be received, or do you like to receive first, then you're happy to payback? You know the drill. Give yourself an honest mark.

Vision

Do you have a plan? Know exactly where you're going? On waking, do you have a clear objective for the day? Yes? Doesn't it make you feel great? What about in 1 year's time? What about 5 years? What about 10 years? What's your vision? Do you know exactly what you want to do? Do you know exactly what you want to achieve? If you're that type of person, you're going to get a high mark for Vision.

I heard a great story once about Neil Armstrong. The story is that he stood and looked at the moon and he said to his mother, 'One day I'm going to go there.' Everybody laughed. He was less than 10 years old and there he was, telling people that one day he'd go to the moon. Space travel didn't exist at that time, never mind travelling to the moon. Of course he continued with his amazing vision. He studied, he worked hard, and he became a test pilot. He was getting closer and closer, pushing the limits. Then he got a chance to join the Space Program. When the Lunar Program was launched, he was one of the very first to enrol. He worked tirelessly every single day, always making sure that he was at the forefront, continuing with his vision. Of course, we all know what happened next. He got the chance to go to the moon, and not only that, he got the chance to be the first person to walk on the moon.

That level of vision, that level of passion and enthusiasm for a clear future is what drives many people. You're going to read a lot more about this during the book, about your vision, about where you want to go.

Of course, many of us don't know what we're going to be doing for the rest of the day, never mind tomorrow, next week or in 1 year, 5 years or 10 years. You may ask, 'Who on earth could possibly know what they're going to be doing in 5 years' time?' There are too many problems out there – too many factors, too many things that you can't control. Is that your way of thinking? Unfortunately you get a lower mark. So give yourself a mark for where you stand with your own personal Vision.

Career

Do you wake up on a Monday morning and shout, 'Yes, it's a work day!' feeling full of energy and excitement about going in to work? Do you love your job so much you would do it for free? Are you lucky enough to feel excited and passionate about your work and career? Then that gets a high mark.

Or, do you wake up on Monday mornings with, 'Oh well it's Monday, great news. That means it's Tuesday tomorrow, closely followed by Wednesday, Thursday, Friday and the weekend – and weekends mean . . . no work'? Unfortunately, some people have a career that they totally dislike. 'I hate doing this.' It's tragic really, but if you know you're in the wrong job, that the thing that you spend most of your time doing is not the right thing for you, then I'm afraid you must give yourself a lower mark. More good news, later on in this book I'm going to show you some fantastic techniques to juice up what you do or to help you find the job that you want to do most in your life. Give yourself an honest mark on the Wheel to reflect your score on Career.

Personal development

Are you the type of person who gets passionate and excited when learning about successful people's lives? Are you passionate about your own personal growth? Do you love to learn? Do you yearn to grow? Do you need to develop? Are you really excited about new things? About learning? About changing? About stepping up? About being a better person? Great news – you're going to achieve a high mark for Personal Development on the Wheel. In fact, here's the brilliant news; you get 2 bonus points just by reading this book! It's important that you recognize you've already started the journey.

Perhaps you're reading this book because you attended a personal development course. Now for your own personal development, ask yourself these bigger questions: 'What was the last thing that I read?' 'What was the last course I attended that I paid for personally?' This is *personal* development. The investment is in your time, in your resources, to take a programme like this and to step up. You make a choice to personally develop yourself, that's what makes the difference. We spend hundreds and hundreds of pounds on our cars, on our own personal appearance, on fabulous holidays. But the biggest return comes from investing our time, energy and resources on our own personal development, our own growth, we see huge benefits paid back.

Give yourself a mark for how you feel about your own Personal Development, not where you think (or hope!) it's going to be in a week's time, a month's time or a year's time; how you feel about it *now*, at this exact moment.

The next stage in the Wheel of Life is to join up all those different pointers. See the example below.

Are you the type of person who **gets up** in the morning and **shouts, 'Yes**.

It's Monday morning,

I've got **so much energy'?**

If you have a perfectly round circle of 10s, I would like to meet you personally, shake you by the hand and buy you a drink and find out how you are doing it. There are very few people who, at this stage, have a perfectly round Wheel of Life. Most of us have a wheel, which is in and out, pointy and disjointed. When you have that type of wheel, is it any surprise that sometimes life is a bumpy journey?

The whole purpose of the Wheel of Life is to identify where the challenges are now, and if you gave yourself a mark of less than 5 in any of the 8 areas, then we've got some work to do. This programme is about addressing those areas now.

There are many reasons why you may have been attracted to this book – maybe to help with your career – then you suddenly realize you have a mark of 3 for your Close Family, guess what? You have an emergency in the Close Family area, and we're going to take actions to fix it right now with this book.

You may have a 10 in Vision.

Ask yourself,

'What gives me that 10?'

What gives you that level of certainty about your Vision that enables you to give yourself a 10? Could that Vision help you in the areas of your Wheel of Life with lower marks?

The Wheel of Life, like most areas of personal development, is not something that you're only going to do once. The next stage is in one month's time, when you should prepare a new Wheel of Life, and repeat the process. Give yourself totally honest marks.

Take the first Wheel of Life you completed, along with your new one. Put one on top of the other, and hold them up to the light. You'll notice that in some areas you have improved. What have you done to achieve that? What actions did you take to change? It may be that another area of your Wheel of Life has started to drop slightly, it's not obvious immediately – but it's there, right in front of you. And that's what this is all about. The Wheel of Life allows you to focus on improvement; it's a continuous process, something to review every single month. It allows you to take action and fix problems before they become too serious.

If you need extra copies of the Wheel of Life then go to our website: www.michaelheppell.com.

Brill Bit

Work towards a balance to achieve a smoother ride in life.

This is a life-changing process for you. It makes such a big difference to the people who take the effort and make the commitment to fill in a Wheel of Life each month. You can do it more often if you wish. Go for balance. Remember – it isn't about getting 10s. It's about getting a wonderful balance.

I've been fortunate enough to meet some amazingly successful people; people who could have 20 out of 10 for Career! Then they share with you some issues surrounding maybe Relationships or Close Family – areas where they need some help. I see people who have incredible methods for dealing with the area of Money, or amazing methods for dealing with Health. Unfortunately they were so concerned about those areas that they ended up in the wrong job, they don't love what they do any more, and their life feels out of sync.

The Wheel of Life is about **getting a balance**; it's about personal growth; it's the foundation **to ensure** you have the **quality of life you deserve**.

Truly brilliant people tend to have a brilliant Wheel of Life. But it doesn't happen by accident. They have a series of tools and techniques to use so that when they are applied, they become brilliant. They're called . . .

2
the

five
characteristics of
brilliant
people

We hold seminars all over the world and ask this question: 'Who do you consider to be brilliant?' The same names come up time and again. People who have truly changed the face of the planet, people who are renowned for their business success. Great sports people, great leaders, sometimes great friends or family members of the audience. When we start analyzing exactly what it is that makes people brilliant, almost everyone agrees on the same set of characteristics. Tens of thousands of people can't be wrong, so here are the five characteristics of the most brilliant people.

1 Positive action

Would you agree that the most brilliant, successful people in our society – the most brilliant successful people throughout history – are positive? I'm sure you will also agree that we tend to be a nation of moaners. I often smile at the thought of it being an Olympic event! Great Britain would win a gold guaranteed.

Just picture it,

as we walk **towards**

the podium to **receive**

our medal we glance

down,

a little **bit disgruntled**,

and comment,

'Well, it's **not very big is it?'**

Why do we behave in this way? Perhaps society dictates we should. Maybe it's so much simpler for us to take the negative route.

I really do believe that *positive action*, more than positive thinking, is the number one cornerstone to making a huge difference to the way that we live our lives. Let me tell you the difference. Positive thinking is great; yes, I'm a fan of it, but it doesn't work all of the time. (Negative thinking – now that works 100 per cent of the time.)

Tony Robbins describes positive thinking as like walking into a garden full of weeds, looking down and saying, 'No weeds, no weeds, no weeds'. What will it do to the weeds? Nothing. It's the *actions* that you take that make the difference.

Brill Bit

Thoughts are things – it's the doing that makes the difference.

You can take this to an extreme. The next time you need to weed your garden, dress in a skin-tight *lycra* suit with a giant 'W' on the front and attach a flowing cape to the back. Take a golden trowel, play 'The Eye of the Tiger' as loud as you can, and pace

into your garden as' 'Weed Man' or 'Weed Woman' shouting, 'Come on you weeds …!' as you attack the weeds full on.

I guarantee in no time at all, you will have got rid of the weeds, your neighbours, friends, family …

Or you might just fancy a bit of full-on weeding minus the costume!

So if we are agreed that it is the actions we take which make the most impact, what are the most important and the most common actions we carry out every minute of every day?

I was told recently that there are 1,250,000 words in the English language. 'Seems like a lot', I said but I'm happy to accept it. Now let's take a look at how we use those words. The words we use in thought, the words we write, the way we communicate, the power of words. How often do we use negative language? Think about it. What is your stimulus response (your immediate involuntary action), when somebody asks, 'How are you?'? You retort with words that seem to be embedded deep within us. You might say something like 'fine' or 'not bad'. Is that the best you can do with 1.25 million to choose from?

Here's a 30-day challenge for you. When asked, 'how are you?' say (you've probably guessed by now). The best word. 'Brilliant'. Now why is that such a great word? Well, first of all, it's very emotive. Second, a word like 'brilliant' makes a difference as soon as you say it. The third thing is the reaction it gets from other people, especially if you have been a 'not bad thanks' person for years and years. Suddenly somebody says, 'How are you today?' and you reply with 'Brilliant! How are you?' That is when you start to get amazing responses. You might be asked if you've just been to a seminar or are you on drugs!

You have got to believe it, *as you say it*. Sometimes it's a bit of a challenge because you may not really feel brilliant. Wouldn't it be great if, for the next 30 days, no matter how you feel, no matter what's going on in your life, if somebody says to you 'How are you?' you reply 'Brilliant, thank you'.

Brill Bit

When you learn new responses, or any new language, you create a new pathway of brain cells. In this case the new pathway of cells is the 'Brilliant' pathway. The more you say it, the easier it becomes and the pathway strengthens. Brilliant!

Later on we'll look at how our brain works and understand what a key ingredient language is.

Use the 'Brilliant' response and you will see something amazing over the next 30 days.

Brill Bit

The 'Brilliant' tool will affect the lives of those around you. Watch as eyes light up when you smile and give a full-on 'Brilliant'. Use it when the skies are cloudy, the traffic is slow, the boss is going mad and the kids are driving you round the bend!

It doesn't stop there, because our choice of words, our choice of language, is vital for achieving brilliance. I'm not one of those people who walks around spouting, 'Yeah, yeah, yeah. Everything's wonderful. Everything's brilliant. Ooh, the world is a wonderful place,' because sometimes it isn't like that. I am a true believer and really passionate about choosing the right words to describe the current situation.

Have you ever heard people say these:

'I'm bored'
'I can't be bothered'
'I feel ill'
'I'm tired'

When you say things like that, guess what starts to happen. You start to become those things. You'll start to feel tired. You'll feel bored. If you say, 'I feel ill' then your brain has a process that will make you feel worse.

If you lived in California it would be really easy. If you felt tired you would just leap up, face the sunshine and shout out at the top of your voice, 'I'm energized!' Stop for a moment and think what would happen if you did that where you live!

So what can we do? How can we change it without feeling that we're faking things?

If you are tired, would it be true to say you could actually 'do with more energy'? And would it also be true that your body has that energy? I sometimes say to people on my live seminars, 'You may feel like you have no energy left. But if I was to say: "The first person to run around the block will get £10,000," I can guarantee that people who'd never run for years could find the energy to go out and have a crack at it!' The energy would materialize because it was always there.

So, rather than say 'I'm tired', you could say 'I could do with more energy.' It's the same thing. It may be a different choice of words, but it's the same thing. Let's take a look at the response that you're going to get from your brain. 'I could do with more energy': the key words here are 'more' and 'energy'. It's a request to your brain for 'more energy'.

Your brain **is like** a filing cabinet; it has references to every time you've used a particular word.

Brill Bit

The more you use a word, the stronger the pathway brain cell becomes. That's going to make a difference to how you communicate using your physiology, your facial muscles, your language, how much your eyes are going to light up, how people are going to feel towards you. They're all going to make a difference.

When we say things like, 'I could do with more energy,' immediately your brain goes, 'Yep, I know how to do more energy.' Your brain will release chemicals, it will change your breathing habits, you will stand in a different way because you will have been given more energy.

If you are the moaney type you might say, 'Well I'm quite happy feeling tired.' Great! If you want to do that, if you want to go through your life feeling tired and run down, then that's up to you. This is a language for people who want to change. This is a language for people who want to be brilliant.

Rather than say, 'I'm bored', why not say, 'This could be more interesting'? You don't have to turn it around and say, 'This is the most incredible, wonderful and interesting thing ever.' I REPEAT you do not need to do that. What you do, very simply, is to say, 'This could be more interesting.' What do you think is going to happen if you say 'This could be more interesting'? Do you think you may find just something in there, just a small shred of evidence to show that the thing that you are listening to, that you are watching, that you are participating in *is* more interesting? Absolutely!

Bonus 30-day challenge

Have a real, what we might call, 'Pity Party'. Write down the different types of negative language that either you hear yourself saying or you hear from other people around you. Write them down. Remember the learning is in the doing, so really do this exercise.

Now, with your list, here is what you are going to do.

Have a look at what is the opposite of the language that you are using. Before, when you said you were 'tired', could the opposite of that be 'energized'? When you were 'bored' could the opposite of that be 'interested'? If you said you 'feel sick', could you 'be healthier'? Start and have a look at the different types of language.

The next part is to say, 'OK, we aren't going to go over the top here, I want brilliant results but what would the truth be?' Sometimes people feel a little bit run down. If you want to feel run down, just start telling people that you are feeling run down. If you want to feel better, you say, 'I could be feeling healthier.' You can do this with some integrity. Say it like you mean it, like you really do want to feel better. Guess what starts to happen? Very very quickly, you'll start to feel better.

If you want **more energy**

and you say

'I could do with more energy**'**,

then you'll soon

get more energy.

Here is a list of some classics and some new language:

I'm tired	I could do with more energy
I'm bored	This could be more interesting
I'm pissed off	I could be happier
The weather is awful	The weather could be better
I'm scared	I could be more confident
This is crap	This could be better
He's a liar	He could be more truthful
I'm freezing	It could be warmer
It's too hot	It could be cooler
I'm broke	I could do with more money

Sometimes though this doesn't work – sorry, could work better! In some areas the next positive action is to use **The power of questions**.

What questions are you asking yourself? What are you saying to yourself every single day? What are the questions going through your head?

Sometimes we say, 'Why is this so boring?', 'Why does that happen?' or 'We can't change this'. What if you were to say things like, 'How could I change this?', 'How could this be more interesting?' Ask a different question – you get a different result.

Brill Bit

Questions are so powerful. When you ask yourself a question your brain has to answer it. It might not think it knows the answer straightaway, but it starts to process finding an answer and it will come.

You have to be very careful about the questions you ask. First, make sure they are positive. Make sure that they are going to demand a response from you. When you ask those questions of yourself, again and again, in a positive way, I guarantee, you'll get positive responses coming back through.

Sometimes when I hold seminars, people say to me, 'Yes, I'm going to do that. I'm going to try and be more positive.' 'I'm going to try and use this language.' They even write down 'I'm going to try harder, I'm going to try to find a way.' There is a word in there which is a very disempowering word; that word is 'try'.

Here's an example. Wave your hand right now, just take your hand and start and wave it. I know it seems silly but go with me on this. If you are reading in a public place you might make some new friends! So go on wave your hand for a moment. OK stop. Don't wave your hand at all. Keep it still. Now try and wave your hand – go on, try and wave your hand. If your hand has moved, that's not trying – that's waving your hand like the first time. Just 'try' and wave it. As you see, 'trying' to do something is the same as not doing it.

'Try' is a weak word.

Brill Bit

If you ever organize a party and someone says, 'We're going to try and be there' then put those people on the 'We won't be there under any circumstances even if it was the last party on the planet' list. When people say 'try', it's a wimp's way of saying they are not 100 per cent committed to doing something.

So now we know that we can change our language; we can change our stimulus responses; we can ask better questions; and there are other words we can eliminate altogether. The final part of this important section of the book is our self-talk. What do we say to *ourselves*? It's very simple to put yourself down. 'Damn, why can't I do this?', 'I am so ugly', 'I am too fat', 'Why am I so stupid?', 'It doesn't work for me', 'Nobody likes me', etc. Of course the more that you do this, the more you believe the self-talk, the more you will start to become like the language that you use. So our self-talk is critically important.

Who controls self-talk? You do. Sometimes it feels a little bit uncomfortable when you have been beating yourself up for so long to suddenly turn around and be a more positive person. Sometimes it feels like you are faking it. Well that's OK because initially we may have to feel that we are faking some of our self-talk, by starting to tell ourselves that we are doing well, telling ourselves we are popular, saying internally and externally that we do feel good about ourselves. The more that we tell ourselves these positive affirmations, the closer we get to being that type of person.

It starts with the language that we use. I'm not saying that you should turn around and yell, 'Yee-ha, everything in the world is wonderful, the sun always shines and it's a most incredible place ever and everything is superb to me, raa-raa-raa-raa-raa,' because people like that could get locked up! All I am suggesting is we can choose how we feel about each given situation.

Review

The first characteristic of being a brilliant person is they take positive actions. With the words they choose, the questions they ask of themselves and the internal language they use.

2 Break out of limiting beliefs

The second characteristic of brilliant people is that they break out of limiting beliefs or they step outside their comfort zones. Things that hold other people back they just seem to smash through again and again.

I heard a great story once about two guys who were at school together. One of them was called Richard and the other one was called John. Richard and John had a plan to start their own school magazine. They talked about it and they talked about it. It was easy to just talk about it, but one day Richard said, 'We're going to have to go and ask the head teacher of the school, if it's possible to start our own magazine.' So they arranged to meet at midday and ask the Principal for permission.

They stood there waiting to go in and all of a sudden John nervously said, 'I'll be back in a moment' and he rushed off down the corridor. After five minutes he hadn't returned so Richard decided he was going to do it anyway. He took the first step out of his comfort zone and started to walk along the corridor.

This was an old-established, very traditional boys' school. As he walked along the corridor, past the portraits of all the other head teachers, he felt butterflies in his stomach. He arrived at the end of the corridor and there on the door a brass plate announced, 'Headmaster's Study'. He knocked and after a moment or two the door flew open and there was the Head, a very tall, very proud man.

At that point, I must say, Richard said he was frightened.
'Yes, what do you want, Richard?' boomed out the voice.

'Well, Sir, John and I were wondering' – no sign of John of course – 'whether it would be possible to start our own school magazine?'

'But we have a school magazine; it comes out each term.'

'Yes, but we want to do this a little bit more often, we want it to be fun, we want it to have jokes in.'

'It's going to be great for our English and it's going to be a great skill for us to learn.'

The Headmaster agreed to it but the rules were: they had to produce it themselves; they had to pay for everything themselves and they had to make sure everyone knew they were publishing it – high risk.

Richard left the office and he found his friend,

'John, where did you go to? What happened? What happened to you?'

John sheepishly stammered, 'Well, I was going to come along, but I, well. I just . . .'

'It doesn't matter – great news – we can do it, but we have to pay for it ourselves, produce it ourselves and take all the risk.'

At that point John started, 'I can't believe it. Oh no, we are never going to get the money. How are we going to copy it?'

'Forget that,' Richard said. 'Let's just write it – we can do it.'

They wrote the first edition of the magazine and managed to copy it with one of those old roller copier machines. They were so excited about it, all covered in ink and ready to distribute their work of art. They went into school the next day and they started to hand out copies of their magazine. One sheet of A4 copied on both sides with all sorts of stories, little anecdotes, some poems and some fun.

Everybody who read it agreed on one thing . . . that it was absolute rubbish. Richard and John found copies lying on the school field, pushed into the back of drawers and thrown on the floor. At that point John immediately jumped back into his comfort zone. But Richard thought about things differently. He asked a better question: 'What can we do to make this work?' They started to ask people good questions about what they would like to read, what they would be interested in. What they found was the things that they were writing about and what people actually wanted to read about, were two different things. They went back to the drawing board and out of their comfort zones again. This time they produced a magazine that everybody loved.

They produced another copy and another copy. Both boys were aged 16 and it came to the day that they left school. Richard had a suggestion for John, 'Let's start our own magazine.' John's response? 'I tell you what, let me think about it and I'll give you a call.'

He never called.

Richard did start his own magazine. It was a magazine for students and it did pretty well. Sometimes they thought that it was going to go bust but within a year they had built up quite a good readership. Richard noticed something; the people who were doing the very best from his magazine were the people who were selling things by mail order. It looked a great way to run a business; the money came in first – you bought the product at a discount and then sent it out. Brilliant! So Richard wanted to get involved with mail order and he decided to sell albums. He had never done it before, so once again it was a big step outside of his comfort zone.

It seemed such a long time since he stood outside of the Headmaster's study. That was easy compared to what he had to do now, setting up deals, buying albums, but once again his business idea was starting to really work. Who should he bump into but his old friend John! It was two years later now.

He said, •John, I can't believe it's you. I'm doing so well. The magazine is doing great but I'm starting to get much more into this idea of doing mail order. We're advertising in other people's magazines and I'm too busy. Do you want to run the magazine?•

John asked •Well, how's it going?•

•Well, you know it could be better; cash is tight but let's go for it anyway. We'll be partners. Do you want to do it?•

Once again, John said, •Richard, I'll give you a call.•

He never called.

Richard didn't worry for long; he was caught in a bit of a predicament. He had a lot of records and there was a postal strike. If he didn't sell that stock, he knew his business would go under. A friend of his suggested there was an opportunity to take a shop on Oxford Street in London above an old shoe shop. They filled it up with records, stood outside and dragged people off the street to go in and listen to the records, buy the records, chill out and have some fun. They did so well those first few days that he saved his business and he liked the idea of record shops. He quickly opened another one and then another two. Richard noticed that the people who were doing really well from the music industry weren't the people who had the record stores; it was the people who owned the record companies.

So once again he moved out of his comfort zone and he started his own record company. Whereas everybody else was signing up a certain kind of act at that time, he signed a guy called Mike Oldfield. A funny little guy who had this great plan to record an album called 'Tubular Bells'. Richard let him go completely crazy with it; he gave him a total free rein and he created something that had never been heard before.

Not only did he take a risk, but he took an amazing calculated risk because it became one of the biggest selling albums of all time and that's a good start for a record company! Not only was he doing well with his other businesses but he was now involved with the record industry and started to expand things. Starting new businesses was easy for Richard now. He got involved with publishing, started to get involved with videos and video games. Business was easy and he needed another challenge.

Who should he bump into? His old friend John! Richard gave him one more chance, 'I'm about to start a new magazine, a brand new kind of magazine, I want you to come and join me.' This was five years later from where they all started together at school. John thanked him for the opportunity and said, 'I tell you what I'm going to do, Richard. I'll give you a call.'

He never did call.

As you can probably guess, Richard went on to do many things, not only with his businesses, but he also started to challenge himself physically. He challenged himself to be the fastest person to get across the Atlantic in a boat. He also set a challenge to be the first person to fly across the Atlantic in a hot air balloon. The first time he failed. The second time he managed to do it. He set a challenge to be the first person to fly across the Pacific in a balloon. Do you remember the first attempt? I watched on TV as the balloon stood up and the sides started to peel off; it had frozen and when it stood up it all came to pieces. For a moment, if you saw Richard on the television, you'd think he wasn't a positive person! He quickly regained his composure after using the 'F' word – not Fantastic, the other one – and he said, 'We'll be back next year. We're going to come back and we're going to do it again.'

Sure enough, one year later, once again massively out of his comfort zone, they attempted the flight again. This time Richard and his team succeeded. They were the first people to fly across the Pacific and, of course, he had a press conference. It was in a big sports hall in Canada, the world's media were there and it was beamed back live to the UK. It was being shown on BBC television that night. There was a man that night sat with his family, he turned to his wife and he said, 'I could have been Richard Branson's business partner.' His wife turned to him, yawned and said, 'Yes, John, I know.' He must have told that story 1000 times about what could have been.

Brill Bit

Who knows what would have happened if John had joined Richard in his business ventures? Who knows what sort of a lifestyle he would have enjoyed? Maybe it wasn't for him. He never gave it a chance to find out. He'll never know. Why? He couldn't break out of his comfort zone – the thing that was holding him back.

So what is it that holds us back? What is it that keeps us inside our comfort zones? FEAR. It's fear that holds us back. Think of fear as a simple acronym for **F**alse **E**vidence **A**ppearing **R**eal.

95 per cent of the stuff that we are **frightened** of is just **false evidence**.

Fear is holding you back. How do we know this? Start by analyzing situations when you've been too frightened to do something. Maybe it's been meeting a new person, or an interview for a job, taking an exam, asking for a pay rise, communicating a new product or a new service. These are moments when we feel anxiety. When we look back, what we thought we were frightened about and what we were really frightened of were two different things.

Brill Bit

I guarantee if you begin to analyze your fears and the things that you really believe are holding you back, you'll notice that 95 per cent of them you just made up. You created them. It was false evidence or it was something crazy that somebody else said.

Let's create some tools right now that you can use to get out of your comfort zone. Here's a simple way to get out of your comfort zone, plus you are going to make new friends and you are going to positively influence some other people's lives.

I would like you, in the next 24 hours, to start conversations with five people you've never met before, five complete strangers. Start talking to them. Make their day. Pay them a compliment. Find out something about them. If you're on the train, talk to the person who is opposite you. If you're on the bus. talk to the person who's sitting next to you. At the supermarket, talk to people in the queue, talk to the person sitting behind the checkout (they definitely need some stimulation!). Talk to someone in a lift. If I walk into a lift with more than two other people I usually say, just as the doors close, 'I suppose you are wondering why I called this meeting?' The reaction is great. If you can get a smile on their face, you get bonus points for this process but it must be five people in 24 hours.

You know what? You are going to enjoy it so much that in the next 24 hours you're going to do another five, and wouldn't it be great if that became a habit? Out there every day positively influencing people's lives by communicating with them. Do you know what's going to happen once you've talked to 50 people? You'll wonder why you were ever scared about communicating with strangers.

You might be sitting reading this now and saying 'Well I do that already. That's the type of person I am.' That's great. Do it bigger, do it bolder and be better. Communicate brilliantly. Talk to the person who you would least expect to have a conversation with. If you go to a party, or to a function, talk to the people you normally wouldn't communicate with.

The next stage is to document times, actually write down and keep a diary of moments when you've broken through the comfort zone, the thing that holds you back. Those limiting beliefs that are there; you know when you've done it. Start keeping a diary. So if you get into a place again, when you are worried, when you think 'Oh, no, what can I do about this?', then you can refer back to that diary and say, 'I've done this before. I know I can do it. Come on!' Use self-talk, use the positive language that we talked about earlier to make a difference for you.

Finally, if you really want to know about bursting out of limiting beliefs, use these three magic ingredients:

1. **Pace**   Increase your pace. Physically move faster, do things quicker and you'll feel more confident about moving out of your comfort zone.

2. **Team**   Work as a team. It's always easier to break out of your comfort zone if you're working with others. Imagine being part of an organization where it's the norm to be out of your comfort zone.

3. **Fun**   The third element is fun. It's much easier to be out of your comfort zone when you're having fun. I recently bought part of a company and sold part of one of my companies and had some big meetings with lawyers. At the end of the meetings, the partner in the lawyers' firm commented on the fun we'd had in the meetings and how unusual this was. 'Most people just sit and worry' he told me.

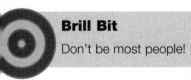

3 Think differently

The third area for all of these brilliant people is that they think differently. If they had the same thinking process as other people, then they'd get the same results. I love this quote from Einstein:

'You can't solve your problems with the same thinking that caused them in the first place.'

Isn't that wonderful?

Understanding how your brain works is the first stage towards having a different way of thinking. Understanding the processes that take place will make a difference.

Many people have talked about left and right brain thinking. I first read about it 15 years ago and I got a closer understanding when I started to study the work of personal development geniuses and psychologists around the world. The first thing that I understood was that the brain has two main hemispheres. The neo cortex, which means new cortex, is the most recently formed part of the brain, and is the part that deals with most of our higher-order thinking.

Two guys, Robert Ornstein and Roger Sperry, in the 1960s, did masses of research into the brain. They discovered that the brain has functions that happen on the left-hand side and control the right-hand side of the body. We also know that we have functions on the right-hand side that control the left-hand side of our body. The Egyptians first discovered this whilst they were building the pyramids. People would get head injuries and whilst treating them they also discovered that the left brain was controlling the right-hand body and the right brain was controlling the left-hand body. Ornstein and Sperry discovered there was a different type of thinking going on in the two hemispheres.

Let me explain. The left hemisphere is responsible for mainly analytical types of thinking: logic, reading, sequence, speech etc. The right hemisphere, by contrast, processes artistic, musical, spatial awareness, imagination, rhythm etc. People frequently make the mistake of saying that the right-hand side of the brain is the creative part of the brain and the left-hand side is purely a logical part of the brain. This isn't true. Recent research suggests that the brain can actually use different parts in different ways and can almost simulate different types of thinking in different parts of the brain. Right now we're going to look at how you get the two parts working together because *that* is when you get true creativity.

Nature is a wonderful thing. We have a left leg and a right leg; a left arm and a right arm; a left eye and a right eye. The way they work best is together.

I don't know if you've noticed, but our education system starts off by being amazingly creative. Young children have a great balance of left brain and right brain activity. I remember when I was in primary school enjoying 'music and movement'. Super creative, leaping around the school hall: with just my underpants on – or was that just my school. We used to do these wonderful activities, 'I'm a lion, I'm a tiger, I'm a spaceman'. We would be so creative and so imaginative. Then things started to change and we began to believe it was stupid to think and act like that. Ugh, what do you want to think like that for?

Our education system says: yes, more left brain, more left brain, more left brain – to the point where we start to measure somebody's intelligence by how good their left brain activity is.

Unfortunately, we leave our education system with wonderfully developed left brains. We would never do that with another part of our body, would we?

Can you imagine starting up the running machine but with just your right leg? 'I'm just doing my right leg tonight.' 'Just my right arm on the weights today, build up that right body.' You would end up with a really strange looking body if only one half of it was fully developed. So why do we do it with our brains?

What about thinking of things in a different way and looking to get a really true balance? Left brain and right brain – working together. That's when you have true creativity.

Michael Flatley was the main source of inspiration behind *Riverdance.* I watched a programme on the TV where Michael Flatley talked about each degree of planning that went into creating the show. First of all, how they had to measure the exact size of the stage, so that the ideas (which were in his head and had not been choreographed at that point) could be put into practice. The right-hand side of his brain, using this wonderful imagination, would be exploring how the dance might feel or look. The left-hand side of his brain would be working out the parameters in which they move. Then they had to think about and measure the exact area where people would be standing; understand the practicalities of getting changed in time between scenes; calculate how the music was going to fit; and ensure the finances would work for putting on the production.

Brill Bit

Creativity comes when both sides of the brain work together.

The brain of three parts

How would you like to know more about your brain and how it works in 99.9999 per cent of the population?

Dr Paul MacLean came up with a wonderful theory about how our brains work and how to process information. For me, this is very exciting because I got a real understanding about how we process information and thoughts. Dr MacLean talks about the 'Triune Brain', or the 'Brain of Three Parts'. He shows our brains in three main areas.

The first area is called the *reptilian brain*. The reptilian brain is at the top of the spine and can only do basic functions such as fight or flight response. In other words, 'Put 'em up', or 'Whoosh I'm out of here'. That's all it's going to do. It was the earliest part of our brain to develop and it cannot do any 'higher-order' thinking: it cannot make creative decisions, it cannot remember things the way that other parts of our brain do but it does have some great uses.

I remember seeing Steve Irwin, the famous Australian crocodile hunter, when he went to catch a croc in this huge pond. He had to catch the crocodile because it had a septic foot. It was in a lot of pain and Steve wanted to catch it to treat it.

If it had been me, I'd have fired a dart from half a mile away and once the croc was fully unconscious, I'd get my full body armour on and with six big mates I'd go in with a metal net wrap it up and drag it out. Not Steve Irwin. His plan was to walk in with half a pig, feed it the pig and then when it was sleepy after a nice big meal, jump on its back. Good thinking Steve! The guy was as mad as a box of frogs! I really love the way that he worked, but his commentary for this task was the most exciting part.

As he walked into this swamp with half a pig, he turned around to the camera crew and said, 'Well, she's in here somewhere, mate. She's an absolute beauty this one but because she's got a really poorly foot, so she's going to be a bit grouchy.' I'm thinking 'Going to be a bit grouchy!' Then he goes on to explain how this crocodile is about 15 feet long and has amazingly powerful jaws that could take your leg off in one move.

As he's getting deeper and walking further into the swamp, I suddenly realize that with him there is a camera crew. Two guys were there filming it, but who was looking after them? What would happen if suddenly the croc leapt out? I'm sure the cameramen had the same thought because there was a little bit of a camera shake!

Steve's getting deeper and deeper and getting more excited and he's saying how she can probably smell the blood around about now. The camera swoops down onto the pig and there it is dripping with blood.

Suddenly they see some movement out of the corner of their eyes and the camera turns around and just at that point this crocodile is coming towards them and Steve throws the pig right into the jaws of the crocodile but she avoids the pig and goes for them! They start running out at that point – they don't want to be hanging about. They run about four or five steps and then have to jump over a two-metre fence. In one bound all three of them leap. Moments later they realize they're safe but, looking back, what was it that gave them the power to move so fast and leap the fence?

It was during that time that the reptilian brain was able to release enough adrenalin into their bodies to give them the energy and the effort to get out of there. You don't want to be using the creative part of your brain at that point. You don't want to be thinking 'Isn't it wonderful that this animal has been around since prehistoric times. Isn't it fascinating how each one of those teeth has hundreds of pounds per square inch of pressure that could just tear your leg off in a second?' You don't want to be doing that; you want to be out of there and fast. That's a great use of the reptilian brain.

What about bad use of the reptilian brain? It could be having an argument with your partner, perhaps stuck in a traffic jam, or when you receive a piece of news and think, 'I wasn't expecting to get that.' Suddenly all hell breaks loose, people start using their reptilian brains to deal with the situation. This is not good for you. Adrenalin that goes into your body, unless it's used say to get out of a dangerous situation, is going to stay. It's going to manifest and cause health problems and stress. I get concerned about this because I know that if people aren't using that adrenalin it can become evident in all sorts of ways: heart disease, strokes, cancers. You don't want that.

So let's get conscious about the way that we use our brains and be aware of the times when we can

'go reptilian'.

How do we choose which part of our brain to use? Paul MacLean talks about the central part of the brain, or the mid brain, which is also known as the *limbic system*. The limbic system processes information such as long-term memory, emotion, habits, your behaviour. In fact, this is the part of the brain that makes you who you are. Your personality, your traits are in the limbic system. And it is your limbic system which filters thoughts.

A thought may come into your head and you have to decide, which way will that thought go? The thought or stimulus goes in to your limbic system where your long-term memory, your emotions, your habits, your behaviours, the things that make you who you are, are housed. The limbic system then asks, 'Am I going to send the thought up to the neo cortex, to the creative, imaginative part of the brain? Or am I going to send it down to the reptilian brain, the part that's going to snap, the part that's going to react, the part that's just going to run away from the problem, run away from the challenge or fight against it?'

It makes that decision at the speed of light. So how can we make a difference to the way our thoughts are processed? Simple.

Train your brain.

You may now be thinking, how on earth can we train our brains when thoughts are being processed at the speed of light?

It's very simple. Start with the small ones. Remember your response to 'How are you today?' When you choose to say 'Brilliant', you're already training your brain for a more positive result. You are training your brain, creating a habit of sending your thoughts up to the creative, imaginative neo cortex. When a situation comes along which is more threatening or serious, your brain is more likely to send your thoughts upwards to the neo cortex. Why? It is used to sending the thoughts that way, every minute of every day.

Brill Bit

Imagine a soccer team. They practise every single day. They practise passing the ball to the midfield players. All they do is kick the ball back to the defenders. The defenders don't do anything with it; they just knock it around to the back of the pitch.

Now it's 3.00 o'clock on a Saturday afternoon, the whistle blows and the game starts. Which way is the ball going to go? The ball is going to get kicked back to the defenders, why, because they practise all week doing that. They don't know any other way; a bit of a boring football match plus it's a match that that team is going to lose. But what if they practised another way every day? When the ball goes to the midfield players, the midfield players practise kicking the ball to the goal scorers. The goal scorers are situated where the exciting part of the game is taking place. Those people are the ones who are going to win.

So, the midfield players, that's the limbic system. The defenders, that's the reptilian brain. The goal scorers, that's the neo cortex, the creative, imaginative part of the brain. By choosing which way we send our thoughts on a consistent basis we can train our brains to deal with different situations in a much more positive way, a much more imaginative way.

Now that you know this, you have joined a very small percentage of the population who understand how their brain works. There's now evidence from MRI brain scans that when people are given the same stimulus, they deal with the information in their brains in different ways. I watched a video of two people: one was a moaner, the other was a very positive person. They did scans of their brains as their thoughts were taking place. With MRI scanning, you can actually see the brain lighting up as it thinks. The positive person, no matter which information they gave him, he dealt with it using his neo cortex, the thinking cap, the creative imaginative part of the brain. The moaner, no matter what piece of information they gave him, he dealt with it using his reptilian brain. With the same information, processing it in two different ways, which one do you think had the better quality of life? It's pretty obvious, isn't it.

Review

We use our brains in many different ways. The more we can train our brains to use the neo cortex, the thinking cap, the easier it is to process information and to get creative output. So, choose how you process your thoughts to get the results you want.

4 Ability to manage stress

The next characteristic of brilliant people is their ability to manage stress, to turn stress into energy. How do they do that? Simple, they have tools and techniques.

Stress is an unavoidable consequence of life. As Hans Selye (who coined the term as it is currently used) noted, 'Without stress, there would be no life.' It's our ability to manage stress that counts. And relaxation is at the forefront.

You need to understand what happens in your brain when you truly are relaxing. Practising relaxation is a key ingredient to being the brilliant person that you deserve to be.

Let's start by looking at how our brainwaves work. Right now, when you are wide awake, your brain is functioning at a level that is known as *beta*. You are wide awake. When we start to relax and we get to a place where we feel very relaxed, very calm, that area is known as *alpha*. As we go off to sleep, we go first of all into a light sleep, and that area is known as *theta* and then when we go into a deep sleep, the area is called *delta*.

Beta – Wide Awake

Alpha – Very Relaxed

Theta – Light Sleep

Delta – Deep Sleep

When we're at our most relaxed, at a point when we can completely rejuvenate ourselves, we are between alpha and theta. That area, which is known as *alpha theta*, is the point you want to aim for. Some people are able to do it very very quickly, very very simply. Some people who practise meditation are able to go there immediately. For most people though, it takes practice.

Brill Bit

Thomas Edison, the greatest inventor of all time, would sit in front of his fire holding a large steel ball. The fire and comfortable chair would help him to relax, but if he relaxed too much, he'd drop the ball and wake up. He taught his brain to hold itself at alpha theta and thought of many wonderful creative ideas at this point.

Watching TV

is not **relaxing**.

Some people say to me 'Oh yeah, I'm great at relaxing. When I'm stressed I switch on the TV. When I sit down in front of *EastEnders*, I feel so relaxed.' When you think about it, you may be relaxed in that you're sitting down, you're not thinking about too much – and let's face it, most TV you don't have to think about. However, to truly rejuvenate yourself, you need to be in a place that gives your brain an alpha theta type of relaxation.

I often hear people make up all kinds of crazy stuff about stress. 'I actually work better when I'm stressed.' 'A bit of stress makes me feel great.'

They get mixed up with *Ustress* (excitement perhaps before a big event, roller coaster ride etc.) and *Distress* (linked with panic, deadlines, worry etc.).

Let me tell you a story about an organization I was working with, which was a marketing company. They were a great organization but the head of this company had a belief that employees worked better when they were stressed. There was a great atmosphere in the office, people could do all sorts of things during the day, but he expected that when a deadline situation came along, they had to pull all the stops out and everyone would stay behind and work rapidly towards achieving that. All that would happen was people would work faster. They weren't working any better. They weren't being more creative. They weren't being more imaginative; they were just working faster. I believe that it's a fallacy to think, 'Yeah, I'm going to work better when I'm stressed.' No, you work faster. Sometimes you can get some adrenalin, sometimes you can get a buzz, but ask yourself: is that conducive towards achieving what you really want to achieve?

So it's very simple. To tackle stress management you must find a way, every day, to relax to the alpha theta level. Listen to a relaxation cd or tape. Learn to relax. Learn to rejuvenate and really give your brain an opportunity to understand information, to process it and get mega creative.

5 Massive action

The next characteristic of brilliant people is that they take massive action. What do I mean by this? Would the people that you judged as being the most successful, as being the most brilliant, sit around and wait for things to happen? Do you think they follow the crowd? Or are they leading the way by making things happen? My observation is that they are the ones who are out there taking massive action every day.

I sometimes have really lively debates with other trainers or people from other organizations who say, 'Massive action is great, but we are interested in getting it right the first time.' 'Getting it right the first time' is a wonderful principle, particularly if you are an air traffic controller (I fly a lot!) or a brain surgeon. Sometimes, in fact for most organizations, my guess is that people would be much happier if they had a massive action atmosphere at work, or a massive action atmosphere at play and an environment where it was ok to sometimes make mistakes.

Why aren't **you getting** out there and **doing things** instead of just talking about it or **watching others** do it?

Picture this, Bill Gates being interviewed by Larry King on CNN. Larry King is really having a go at Bill Gates and forcing him to answer some pretty tricky questions. Bill Gates thinks he is let off the hook with an easy one.

'What's the secret of your success?' asks King.

'We were at the right place at the right time,' answers Gates. Of course, Larry King isn't happy with that answer.

'Well that's not true,' says King, 'Lots of people were at the place at the right time. But come on, you are Microsoft, you are the biggest on the planet at this stuff. What is it that you did?'

'Well I guess we had a vision for the future for the home computer, for the desk top PC.'

'Yes, you had a vision,' King interrupts him, 'but yours was smaller than most of the competition. So come on Mr Gates, really what was it that made the difference?'

'Well I think it must be down to the quality of our product.'

'It certainly isn't that,' King answers. Wow! By now Bill Gates is feeling a little bit uncomfortable, so Larry King pushes him one more time.

'Come on Mr Gates, what is it that really made the difference? Why is Microsoft number one? Why are you the biggest on the planet by far? Why do 90 per cent of PCs run Microsoft?'

Bill Gates turns and looks at him with total certainty and says, 'We are the ones who took massive action.'

Larry King realizes he's finally on to something and he wants more. 'Can you give me an example of that?'

Bill Gates shares a story about the time when they wanted to become the operating system for IBM and one day they got a phone call saying, 'Come down and show us the work you are doing.' They were there 4 hours later and that included a 2-hour flight.

This was not a group of people who were hanging around. They immediately got on a plane and flew down there and spent as long as it took with the people from IBM. Of course, history shows that because they became the operating system for IBM, they continued to go from strength to strength, becoming the biggest on the planet.

Massive action = Massive results

Brill Bit

I recorded a Time Management Programme called 'Time for Time – Time Management Without the Bull'. One of the most popular parts of the programme is the '$100,000 idea'. The $100,000 idea comes from a story about Charles Schwab.

Charles Schwab, when he was alive, was one of the richest men on the planet, he was the most successful man on the planet. He was running a huge steel empire. One day somebody came to him and requested 'Mr Schwab, I would like to give you an idea and I would like you to use it for one month. At the end of that one month you just pay me whatever you think it was worth.' In the eyes of Schwab it looked like a fair deal. At the end of one month

▶

he thought the idea was worth $100,000, the equivalent of many millions of dollars now.

What was the idea? Simple: at the end of each day write down the five most important things you should do tomorrow. What's the real secret? When you get up that day you make sure those five things are done. Whatever it takes, do those five most important things. If you only get through four, don't sweat it. Number one on the list for the next day is already taken. Actions like that to get things done – that's what makes the difference.

Review

Take massive action.

Massive action =

Massive results.

Even with those five characteristics brilliant people have another ingredient that makes them leaders in their field, they practise . . .

3

brilliant
goal-setting

Time to set some goals. Already? But I don't know what I want. EXACTLY!!!

This is more exciting than you can imagine because you're going to do most of the work and see most of the results over the next 90 days. Why 90 days? It's long enough to get some serious work done but it's short enough to see some results very quickly.

I want to share with you first some fundamental parts of goal-setting that I believe make a massive difference. As you read in the introduction, I'm not a fan of SMART goals. If you already know about these, then the first thing I'd like you to do is forget about them. SMART goals (Specific Measurable Achievable Realistic in a Timescale) are great for outcome setting for individual tasks but I have yet to meet a person who has achieved a major vision through using SMART goals.

I want to talk to you about a more powerful goal-setting technique using the three P's. The three P's are very simple. When you set goals, first of all they need to be **P**ersonal. Second, they need to be **P**ositive. Third, they must be set in the **P**resent tense.

When I say a goal has to be personal, it will include the big 'I'. Organizations can have goals, that's great. Shared goals for an organization are exciting; shared goals for a couple are stimulating; shared goals for a family are stirring – but right now we're talking about YOU and what is going to make a difference to you and your life. Sometimes that sounds a little selfish. OK, maybe it's time for you to be selfish here.

Brill Bit

When it comes to setting goals, you are going to tune into a radio station called WIIFM, that's:

What's In It For Me?

When you set a goal, it's going to start off with the word I. Such as – I am, I have. Really concentrate on thinking what is it that's going to make a difference to *you* when you set these goals.

The second 'P' is that a goal must be positive. I covered positive language earlier, so you should already have an understanding of how this works. Choosing the right words is absolutely critical at this point to make sure that you get the right affirmation in your mind in order to achieve the goal. Let me give you an example. Once somebody said to me, 'I have my goal. There it is. What do you think of that, Michael?' They showed me the goal, which read, 'I am no longer in debt.' What is the key word in that sentence? It's *debt*. You may be thinking, 'Why should that make a difference? That's a great goal. They want to get out of debt and they're being positive about it. It even sounds like it's in the present tense.' Positive language means that we would choose a different word. The different words I suggested were 'financially free': 'I am now financially free,' or 'I am financially free, now' – whichever feels best. 'I'm financially free' is much better than 'I am no longer in debt.'

Remove **negative language** whilst goal-setting and focus on making it **very positive**.

The third area is to set a goal in the present tense. See it as if it has already been achieved. This seems to be a crazy idea to a lot of people. Why would I do that? Could I not say, 'Well, one day I will be financially free' or 'I will be financially free in two years' time'? When you set a goal in the present tense, your subconscious starts working towards achieving the goal.

By setting **a goal in** the **present tense** you create **'Gestalt'**.

Gestalt is a very powerful driving force that can change the speed at which you achieve a goal. Gestalt is your brain's way of wanting to create order. If you were to lie on a sunny day and look up at a blue sky and see the clouds rolling past, it wouldn't be long before you started to imagine other things those clouds might look like. You might say, 'Oh look, there's a ship' or 'Doesn't that one look like old Uncle Albert?' The reason for this is that your brain is making sense of an image.

When you create a goal in the present tense, your brain says 'OK, if that's how things have to look, sound and feel, what do I have to do to make that happen now?' This is why a goal will happen so much faster if you set it in the present tense.

Here's an example of the person who I really believe was the greatest ever goal-setter – Muhammad Ali.

Muhammad Ali **was** the
Ultimate Goal Setter.

Do you remember what Muhammad Ali would say? Do you remember the affirmation he would use? Four simple words,

'I am the greatest'.

Brill Bit

What did Muhammad Ali say before he was the greatest? 'I am the greatest.'

What did he say when he was the greatest? 'I am the greatest.'

What does he say now when he's no longer the greatest? 'I am the greatest.'

The perfect affirmation.

Think about the phrase, 'I am the greatest.' Is it personal? Is it positive? Is it in the present tense?

To be the greatest, Muhammad Ali did more than that. Ali would set goals in an altogether different way. Do you remember in pre-fight press conferences when he would turn to his opponent, look them in the eye and then make one of his famous predictions? Ali would say, 'You're going down in the second minute of the third round.' He would say it with such certainty and such belief that even though his opponent would say 'Yeah, right!', he knew that he was in trouble.

After the press conference, Ali would then do something very interesting. He would go back to his hotel room, or back to his home, lie down and relax from head to toe. Then he would start to use his imagination. Does this sound familiar from anything else in this book? In his imagination he would see the press conference just as it had been. He would see himself make that prediction, but then he would start to visualize the days and weeks ahead and see himself build up to the fight. He would see himself doing amazing training; he would imagine himself preparing and getting stronger and better than the other guy. He knew if his opponent was up at 5.00 am running, then he'd be up at 4.00 am. He envisioned himself during his sparring sessions, getting bigger and stronger.

Then he would imagine the day of the fight. He would arrive outside of the stadium and when he got out of the car, the crowd would be chanting only one name. He would hear it repeated over and over again: 'Ali, Ali, Ali . . .' He would intensify the image. Increase the feeling. Bring it closer to him, imagining and feeling every single word, every single emotion that went with it.

Then he would see himself go into the dressing room and feel the bandages go on to his hands, he would feel the gloves go on and see himself standing strong. Then they announced his name as he walked out. In his mind he sensed the crowd going crazy, screaming just for him. Only his name would be screamed; everybody is on his side.

Then he would get into the ring and look across the crowd, seeing every person screaming his name. He would hear it over and over again, intensifying it, increasing the volume, increasing the emotion: 'Ali, Ali, Ali, Ali'. Then he would turn to his opponent and see him shrink small. They would touch gloves and they would start to fight.

He would then visualize each round – mentally rehearsing the outcome he wanted. He would see the first round exactly as he'd planned it, exactly as he'd mentally rehearsed it. Connecting, brilliant blows, doing the famous Ali shuffle, floating like a butterfly, stinging like a bee!

Then he would visualize the second round, even stronger, even greater, intensifying every moment. Then came the third round and, more importantly, the second minute of the third round. At that moment – boom! He would connect with his opponent with an almighty punch, then see him go down. When his opponent fell, Ali would imagine standing over him and hearing the referee making the count – 'One, Two, Three, Four, Five, Six, Seven, Eight, Nine – you're out!' At that point, when he knew that he had won, he would freeze-frame the image and surround it in brilliant white light. He called this image his 'Future History'.

Never again would he consider an outcome other than his future history. All the time that he trained, he would see his future history. Every time anybody asked him about the fight, his future history is the image he would see. Every morning when he woke up, he would visualize his future history. Every night when he went to bed, his future history is the image that he would visualize. It was a future that he was so certain about, it was as if it had already been documented by the historians.

With that level of certainty, when it came to the day of the fight, guess what would happen? His opponent would be knocked out in the second minute of the third round, just as he'd predicted.

That's how to set goals. Would Ali have been as successful if he had been taught to set SMART goals? 'OK Muhammad, make them specific, make them measurable, achievable, realistic and with a timescale!'

Ali created a belief and a passion and brought it very much into his whole physiology so every moment he lived it; every moment he ate it; every moment he breathed it; every moment he felt it. With that level of certainty, and with that level of passion, you can achieve anything, anything that you put your mind to.

To create that level of intensity requires passion and a need to make a goal a 'must'. Here's your homework. Right now focus on the areas that are important to you. Think clearly about what exactly you want to achieve. To begin with, you're going to set some short-term goals. By this I mean things that are going to happen in the next 90 days. I also want you to have a look at where you want to be in one year; remember, that is only four batches of 90 days. Then think about where you want to be in 5 years and where you want to be in 10 years. Ten years is a long time and the only limit should be your own imagination. Remember this brilliant quote from Michelangelo:

'The **greatest** danger for most of us is not that our aim is **too high** and we miss it, but that it is **too low** and **we reach it.**'

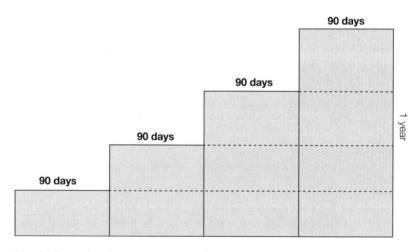

Think about that for a moment.

In 10 years, you will have grown and developed massively. You could do whatever you choose to; you could be anywhere that you want to be. Just break it down into 90-day programmes, 90 days of doing the right actions. Do this and the 90-day chunks will start to build. Your daily actions build up and you'll see yourself step up, step up so much that after three or four batches of 90 days, you're going to say: 'Wow. Look what have I achieved!'

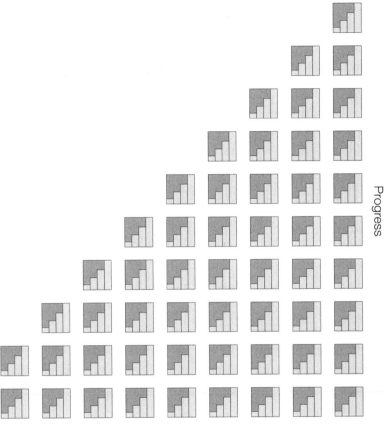

Progress

1 to 10 years

It will be like a boat going through a lock system; every 90 days you get higher and higher and higher towards achieving that goal. After 10 years you'll have travelled so high, you'll be amazed how far you have come.

So get practical and plan your first batch of 90 days. After doing this, you'll see how easily you can plan your first year, the next 5 years and 10 years of this exciting new journey. Start by looking at the actions you have to take right now.

First question: which areas in your life do you want to set goals in? Remember when we first started, we looked at The Wheel of Life (p.11). Eight different key areas in life. Some of the areas flagged up challenges where you knew you had to take action right now. They are the first areas to work on. Look carefully at your Wheel of Life. If you have a low mark in any area then you must set a goal there. It's an absolute must. The reason why? That area is holding you back, it's holding you back from getting the balance in your life that you deserve. A balanced wheel is the foundation. You will find it difficult, so set big stretch goals later unless you have a balance first. Then set a goal or two in each section of your Wheel.

Do you have career goals? Do you have some areas within work where you say: 'Yes. I would really love to achieve that. That's where I want to be. This is how much money I want to be earning within my career. This is how many sales I want to be making. This is how many people I want to serve. This is the type of position that I want to have within this organization.' If so, you can create goals around your career.

What about within your relationships? What type of relationships do you want to have with people? Where do you want to be? How do you want people to view you? How do you want to be seen as a friend? How do you want to be seen as a partner? How do you want to be seen as a parent, an auntie, uncle, son or daughter? Could you have a goal in those areas as well?

What about your health? Do you want to make a difference to your health, to the way that you feel about yourself and the levels of energy that you have?

What about the things you really want? Do you want a particular car? Do you want to go on great holidays? Do you want to go and experience things that you could probably only have dreamt about?

Start to think about the things that really excite you, that really juice you up. Take a moment to write down a few ideas. Write down all the different things that come to mind with those areas. Think about the parts that might be missing from your life – what are they? How are you going to fill them in? Remember to raise your game here. Some are going to be short-term goals, others are going to be long-term goals. Stop reading for a moment and write a long extensive list. Go for it!

Right now, you should have your list. There will probably be too many things on the list, so read through them and ask, 'What do I *really* want?' You can identify the things that you *really* want because these are the ones where you can wax on for hours about the reasons why and the difference it will make in your life. What are the things that are going to drive you as you look at your list? Then make sure you have a balance. To have goals only in one area of your life will quickly become unfulfilling.

Excellent. Now you have a list of goals written down in a positive, personal and present tense. You have made great strides in attacking the areas on your Wheel of Life where you had lower scores and you are beginning to formulate a 90-day plan to get a quick start on achieving your goals. You are heading towards brilliance rapidly. The foundations are laid so if you are ready it's . . .

time to be
brilliant

When Sydney won the Olympics for the Year 2000 it was an exciting time for Australia. I had an opportunity just recently to work in Sydney and Melbourne. Particularly in Sydney, as I was meeting people, I realized that there was a unique energy and excitement in the air. People were excited about what was happening with their country. Businesses are booming. Tourism is going through the roof. I asked if they could put their finger on what it was that had made the difference. Several put it down to an exact moment: the moment when they actually knew that they were going to be hosting the Olympics in the New Millennium.

I started to talk to people and asked many questions. I was fortunate to be introduced to the guy who was the Lighting Director for the Sydney Olympics and asked him about the Opening Ceremony. I don't know if you've had a chance to see the Opening Ceremony but it was the most spectacular thing I have ever seen, for any event staged, anywhere. They had more colour, more excitement, more passion, more visual effects, more sound effects, better lighting and better fireworks. Everything was produced to the highest degree – it all came together amazingly tastefully and it worked so well.

I asked the Director about how they planned an event like this and what it was that made such a difference. He said:

> 'Michael, it started years before the event, all of the people who were going to make it happen, the creative team, came together. The Chief Executive of The Sydney Olympics, Sandy Hollway, walked into the room. He looked at us and he said, 'This is the brief for the Opening Ceremony of the 2000 Olympics. I would like you to get footage of every Olympics there has ever been. I would like you to obtain videos; I would like you to find books; I would like you to acquire photographs; I would like you to unearth old audios; I want you to interview people; I want you to find out what was it that made these previous events as exciting as they were. Then I want you to take the very best, the most exciting, the most emotive and the most passionate of each event. Then bring all of that information together. Increase it to the power of 10 and that is your starting point!'

My new friend concluded:

> 'Michael, we sat there with the hairs on the back of our necks standing on end. We knew we were about to create history. We knew that we were going to do something which had never been done before. We were so excited. For the next five years the excitement was just building all the time. We had to invent new technology to support our ideas. We wanted to do things that had never been done before and because of that excitement, because of that passion, because of that leadership, we were able to create an Opening Ceremony that has never been seen before. Not only that, but the whole Olympics continued to follow that same theme. We had the best transport system, it was the most organized Olympics for the athletes and the press, it was the cleanest, it had the best quality – everybody agreed that Sydney stepped up to the next level and created something which was truly brilliant.'

Why did it happen? How did it happen? Think about it! The days of doing a good job have gone. It is no longer good enough to be 'good' any more. In fact, I often start off presentations with companies when we are working with them presenting in-house programmes with, 'I've done my research and the good news is that you're good.' The delegates will usually cheer here, but I continue, 'But there is some bad news. The bad news is you are good. And doing a good job just isn't good enough any more.'

But it doesn't end there. It seems that other cities in Australia are keen to get on the Brilliance train. Harry Nicolaides was the concierge at The Rydges Hotel in Melbourne. I was fortunate enough to meet him on a recent trip and he touched my life in many ways. First of all, Harry is an exceptional character who is so easy to get along with and has many tales to tell about his experience and life as a concierge. However, Harry's goal of offering 5-star service in every available way was brought to the forefront of my attention with this one gesture. As you would expect, Harry arranged for a short sightseeing tour of the city with key points marked on the map, the names of the Maître D in restaurants, free passes for some of the key sights and telephone numbers of cab firms and tram timetables. This is what Harry does best; making sure that your every need is met. However, it's his attention to detail that really inspired me.

On the second day of our stay, Harry noticed my Events Producer walking through Reception and asked why I wasn't with him. He explained that he was going to the venue where we were doing our training the next day and then I was going to relax next to the pool for a couple of hours. Immediately Harry's mind began to think of ways to improve my relaxation, and with his compliments, he sent a waiter with an ice-cold bottle of beer and a copy of his book *Concierge Confidential*. His timing was impeccable, as I had just begun to fidget and look for something to do.

The book gives tales of brilliance and service beyond the call of duty. Later I read how Harry looked after politicians, enabled hats to be repaired in time for the Melbourne Cup, and dozens of tales of intrigue and skulduggery around his hotel.

Here's how brilliance benchmarking works. Imagine a race is about to begin – the Men's Olympic 100 m. How much faster does the winner have to be than the second-placed runner to take the gold medal? In Athens 2004 the difference between first, second and third was one hundredth of a second.

Now what sort of difference did that make to the first three in the minutes, hours, days and months that followed? Well, the winner gets a gold medal. Oh, and millions of dollars in sponsorship, then there's the opportunity to work with the best trainers and have the best equipment and not forgetting the prospect of being able to run in any race meeting anywhere in the world – everyone wants the Olympic champion.

Take a moment to think about the ones who came second and third. They missed out on a gold medal and all those rewards by one hundredth of a second. They spent 10 years preparing for that moment and missed it by a split second.

The good news is you are probably not an Olympic athlete and that's good news because there is room at the top for everyone who reads this book. But you have to know the rules.

Let's take a look at the scale on the left showing the results people get versus the effort they put in. As you can see on the base-line you have no results, nothing at all is happening. Just above that base-line you have a POOR job. Of course, if you do a poor job, the results you would expect to get would be poor. We don't want to do a poor job so let's go to the next level. The next level after poor is doing a GOOD job. As I said before, who wants to do a good job? Not me, because as you can see by the diagram, when you do a good job these days, what type of results are you going to get? No, not good! If only you were so lucky! You do a good job and you actually get POOR results. How do I know that? Because if you do a poor job you get NO RESULTS – you are out of business, redundant or barely surviving. Can you imagine if you were running a hotel, managing a restaurant or co-ordinating a mail order company and you were consistently doing a poor job, how long would you last? Not very long at all. So, if doing a poor job means you are out of business, it makes sense that by doing a good job you will get poor results. This can be a little disheartening but the examples are everywhere.

When I stay in a hotel, I walk into reception, check in, go to my room and the minimum I would expect is that the room should look absolutely immaculate. It should be clean. The towels should be neat. The bed should be made with well tucked-in sheets. The curtains should be symmetrical and the remote control should work for the TV. This is standard stuff. Not for a moment am I thinking that because this all checks out, that they've done a great job. The minimum expectation I would have is that they would have done all that and more. Why? Because good is the minimum expectation of people these days. Your customers are expecting more and so are your family. So why do a good job when we end up getting poor results?

Good is the **minimum expectation** of people these days.

What is the next stage? The next stage is to go even higher than good (we were talking about this word earlier) by doing a FANTASTIC job. When we do a fantastic job, we would hope to get fantastic results, but look at the model. We do a fantastic job and we get good results. Ah ha! Has the penny dropped?

Many people and organizations spend their time working somewhere between doing a poor and a good job. Every so often they peak towards fantastic. The results come back and they are good, so what happens? They get disheartened and drop right down to where they were before doing a good or a poor job. This can be frustrating for many people. You work so hard, do a fantastic job and just get good results. Check your pay slip, are you getting paid too much?

I used to do a huge amount of work with charities, as my background was working as a fundraiser for several different organizations. They would tell me how they'd just had a 'fantastic' campaign. I would ask them, 'What was the purpose of the campaign?'

'We want to bring in money, we want to help people, and we want to do our work, so we need a lot of money in the organization.' Then I would ask them the big question, 'How much money did you raise?' Often they would say, 'Well the results were good.' Then the organizations would start to justify good results by saying 'Think about the awareness that we gained for the organization. Think about the way that people viewed us.'

At the end of the day, they did a fantastic job but the money – the thing that they wanted to bring in that was going to change the organization, that was going to help their cause – was only good.

So looking at that model, is there anywhere else you can go? There is and it is a tiny fraction; it's just a small difference. If you were to visualize it it's only a few millimetres between fantastic and the next level which is called BRILLIANCE! And that is the key with this book. True success and happiness is about not just doing a good job, not even doing a fantastic job; it is about doing a BRILLIANT job!

True success
is about doing a **brilliant** job!

Brill Bit

Brilliance is about pushing that little extra level, going just one further step, that extra mile. It's about caring more, understanding more, researching more, delivering more and by achieving that you'll do a brilliant job. Put in the effort that others don't.

Here is the most exciting part of the whole process. When you do a brilliant job you don't get fantastic results, you get brilliant results! The rewards are brilliant, the effect on others is brilliant, your quality of life is brilliant. I know it's not fair, but it's true.

If you understand the power of this concept, you'll immediately say, 'That's where I want to be. That's where I want to be in the areas that are the most important in my life.' You will want to do a brilliant job and receive brilliant results. However, the energy you have to put in to being brilliant is huge, so this area must be vitally important to you or you will not give the commitment, energy, passion and enthusiasm that will be needed in order to achieve brilliance.

When I first began to understand this concept I got very excited. Personally, I realized there were two main areas in my life where I wanted to do a brilliant job. Where being fantastic wasn't going to be good enough; where being good was just going to be shocking; and where being poor was a thought I couldn't even contemplate.

Firstly I wanted to be brilliant at being a Dad. I have two great kids and I realized that being a great Dad was going to be one of the most important things, if not *the* most important thing I could do in my life. The second was I wanted to be brilliant at the work that I do and the third was to be a brilliant husband.

Being a brilliant Dad

It's easy to say, isn't it? It is one of those things that just trips off the tongue, 'Yeah, I want to be a brilliant Dad (or Mum),' and everybody agrees: 'That's a great idea. What a wonderful plan.' Then you study the actions that you need to take.

I'd like to tell you a story, and it's a personal story. I'm not making any apologies for this because at the end you'll see how you can apply this in many areas of your life as well. The reason I'm so excited about telling you this story is because I have seen the results week after week, month after month, year after year since I did one small thing in a brilliant way.

When my daughter was 6 years old, Valentine's Day was just around the corner. I remember thinking it might be a nice idea to get my daughter, Sarah, a Valentine's card. I did. It was the night before Valentine's Day. I was driving home, I was weary, I'd been working very hard and I pulled into a service station and went into the small shop. I remember standing looking at the depleted choice of cards that was available. There was one card that I felt was suitable. I took it home and wrote 'Happy Valentine's Day. Have a great one. I think you are wonderful', and tucked it under Sarah's pillow. The next morning she woke up. When she opened the card she looked at it, said 'Oh, that's nice.' She put the card on her shelf and went to school. Within a week the card had gone. You and I both know that it was a good job but the results, quite frankly, were poor.

Over the next year I started to get an understanding of what true brilliance was all about. I noticed Valentine's Day was coming up again and I now had a real commitment to being a brilliant Dad. I started to think – what would a brilliant Dad do? He wouldn't be standing in a service station the night before looking for a card for his daughter; he would get a card in good time and it would be a card that was important to her.

I started by talking at length to Sarah to get an understanding of what was important to her at that time. There were two main things. One was kittens and the other one was the pop group Steps. She loved the idea of getting a kitten and she loved listening to Steps and doing their dance moves. Next day I found a telephone number on a Steps CD, I called the Steps marketing people and asked them if they had a Steps Valentine's Card. The reply came, 'No I'm sorry we don't, but thank you very much for the idea.'

'OK,' I replied, 'do you have any new things available?'

'Yes we do. We've got some new merchandise which is going to be available for their tour which starts in the next couple of months.'

I was so excited about the fact they were going on tour, but it transpired it was a sell-out. The kind chap in the Steps office told me that, on the following Friday, four new dates were going to be announced, one in London, one in Manchester, one in Glasgow and one, locally to me, in Newcastle upon Tyne. Tickets would go on sale at 9.00 am!

I made a commitment to get tickets and formed a plan on how I would acquire them. There are two ways you can buy tickets. Call the credit card hotline – take three telephones and call continuously, only to find out when you arrive at the concert that the tickets are miles from the stage! Or, the best way to get great tickets is to go and stand in the queue.

So that Friday morning I was up at 5.00 am, drove down to the Telewest Arena in Newcastle, walked around the corner and there in front of me, at 6.00 am were 500 kids all waiting to buy Steps tickets. Remember this is right at the beginning of February so it's really cold. Their Mums and Dads were standing around freezing cold but not the kids, they were dancing around a big 'Ghetto Blaster'.

I thought for about 2 seconds and made my mind up to be a kid. I jumped into the middle of the crowd. We were singing the songs, having a great time, and the hours passed very quickly. Eventually they opened the box office. I remember getting to the front of the queue and saying, 'I need two tickets which have a great view but I don't want them to be so close to the front that my daughter will be scared about the crowds.'

'Have a look at this,' said the lady in the box office as she produced a seating plan. She showed me two tickets which were on a slightly raised platform about 20 metres from the stage (you don't get tickets like that by calling the credit card hotline!). I took the tickets and gave myself a mental mark on the brilliance scale. I had done better than a good job, but it still wasn't brilliant, yet!

The next thing I had to do was find the right type of Valentine's card. After I'd been to five or six shops, eventually I found a lovely card that had wonderfully cute kittens on the front. I wrote a little note inside saying, 'Sarah, would you like to go on a date with me on May 21?' I popped the tickets inside and then realized there was one more thing I needed to do.

When we had been on holiday the year before, Sarah had fallen in love with a smell she found in a perfumery. It wasn't the nicest smell for me, it was what I would call an 'old man's' aftershave. Every day she used to spray this stuff on me as we walked past the local shops. She liked the smell. I looked around my local town to see if I could get it. Unfortunately I couldn't find it anywhere so I had to drive to Newcastle just to get a sample bottle and ask them to spray it into the card. I put the tickets in the envelope, sealed it up, wrote her name and address on and put it in the post. Why did I put it in the post and not underneath her pillow? Because kids love to get stuff in the post!

The morning of Valentine's Day arrived. Sarah came downstairs, ambled to the front door and then with a big huge smile on her face she picked up the post and said, 'Oh . . . two Valentine's cards for me!' As her Dad, I'm thinking who was the other one from! The first was from an elderly relative; she looked at it, put it on the shelf and that was it.

Then she opened the next one. As she opened it she immediately got an anchor. The anchor was, 'I can smell holidays.' A big smile appeared on her face. Then she took the card out of the envelope and she looked at the front and there was the picture of those beautiful, cute kittens. Remember that kittens are number one on her important list at that time. She was going on and on, 'Oh, look at the kittens. Oh wow, they're so sweet.' In fact, she was so busy looking at the kittens that the tickets fell onto the floor. She opened the card and read the words out loud, 'Would you like to go on a date with me on May 21?' Sarah looked around at me and said, 'Oh Dad, this must be from you. What are you up to? Come on Dad, what is it?'

I said, 'Sarah, have a look on the floor.' She looked down on the floor and she picked up the tickets. Her little mouth dropped open. She got so excited her legs started to go, her arms started to shake, her eyes became as wide as saucers. She was shouting 'Wow! Are we really going to see Steps?' 'Yes, we're really going to go, we're really going to go.'

That day, she took the tickets and the card to school and showed everybody. Luckily they came home. Then she made a countdown to Steps chart and started to learn all the dance moves and the songs (again!).

It got to the night of the concert. We drove down to Newcastle, she was so excited but also a little bit nervous. We walked in and started to move closer towards the front. Every time one of the security people stopped us they would check our tickets, point towards the front and say, 'Keep on walking, keep on walking'. We got closer and closer and closer to the front and Sarah's grip on my hand got tighter and tighter. When we got close to the stage, they pointed along a line of chairs and sure enough there they were, slightly raised at the front of a platform. We moved to the two centre seats – just for us! We watched an amazing show that evening – it was as if the whole concert was just for us. Sarah was jumping in the air and we had a night of dancing and singing.

We both had a brilliant time but the real true moment came for me when we were on the way home. We were in the car and Sarah turned to me and said, 'Daddy, today has been the best day of my life.' I'll always remember it because she said it with such sincerity, such belief that it truly was one of the greatest days of her life. It will stay with me for ever, but guess who else it stays with? Every time we drive past the arena, Sarah talks about the time when she went to see Steps and Dad gave her the card with the kittens on. She still has the card now years later and she's always telling her friends about this great evening, the card and the smell and the seats.

What's the message? Really simple: if being brilliant at something is important to you, make an honest judgement about where you are on the scale right now. Are you currently doing a poor job? Are you currently doing a good job? Or are you currently doing a fantastic job? Whichever one of those levels you find yourself on, the message is simple. Step up!

The message is simple. Step up!

You must step up to the next level. Once you decide to step up to that next level, do whatever it takes to achieve it – this is when you are going to reap the rewards. You don't just get good rewards, you don't get fantastic rewards, but you'll get brilliant rewards. No matter how you measure it, you'll get brilliant rewards, it's almost not fair.

There are so many examples that we can read and study today, about people who have decided to step up to be brilliant. One of the most exciting and inspirational stories is about Ellen MacArthur, who decided that one day she'd be one of the, if not *the*, best yachtswoman on the planet. What she did was incredible. It started when she was 8 years old and she went on a sailing holiday with her aunt. She said, 'Wow, I love this' and it started a passion for sailing. She started to practise and study sailing, to get a deeper understanding. She took every single opportunity she could to sail. It didn't stop there. That would have been doing a good job. She wanted to be at the next level. To do that, she needed commitment. She used to save her money every day; she wouldn't have any lunch. Why? She would save her lunch money every day so she could do more yachting, plus she was saving for her own yacht. Eventually she bought her own yacht but quickly outgrew it. She wanted another yacht that was even bigger and better so she could push it and herself to the limits.

When she got it, she had to work on it for three months to make it seaworthy. In order that she could invest so much into that yacht, she would sleep underneath it every night to save money and still escape the elements. That level of commitment, that level of passion, that level of determination pushed her to a point of brilliance.

Did she get the rewards for that? There is no doubt she did. She already has an MBE. People around the globe would talk with such reverence of Ellen MacArthur because she is seen as one of the true leading lights of the yachting world. She can pick her crew and work with the very best. She has won competitions, she has become internationally famous, people all over the world want to hear her speak, they want to know her story and now she is in a position when she can demand the sponsorship she needs to help her fulfil her dreams. People now come to her wanting to invest in what she's doing, in her determination, in her brilliance. So what made Ellen so successful?

It is evident that Ellen's vision, goals and passion have taken her to unbelievable heights. These skills are definitely needed to be brilliant at sailing, but can they be applied to brilliance in other areas too?

Here is your next task. Take some time to think and reflect on what you would like to be brilliant at. If you are already good in an area, do you want to be better in that area? If you have a passion for something, do you want to move up to brilliance? Start to think now. Once you get commitments, write them down. Immediately you think maybe of 10 things. A word of warning – the level of passion, enthusiasm and the amount of work that you are going to require to be brilliant will mean you need to narrow your list down to just two or three things at most. Do not ask 'How?' at this moment in time, and *do not* consider in any detail how you are going to do it. Further on in this book we'll be addressing all of this. First, we are going to have a look at getting rid of parts that hold you back, creating a vision and putting together a plan on how you can truly step up to the level that you want to be on. It's the secret of how to be brilliant – it's about taking action now.

You may also be thinking, 'I'm going to do that. I'll start next week.'

Remember, massive action equals massive results. So do it now! Make a commitment to the key areas in your life where you want to be brilliant right now.

Is it done? If it isn't, stop reading, go back and do it right now. This is important. This is going to change your life. Just reading will not make the difference to your life but taking action and writing things down will. This book is about taking action, so if you haven't done it – do it now.

So now you have decided on a maximum of three areas in which you want to be brilliant, give yourself a pat on the back. You are already a big part of the way there! Think for a moment about those areas. I guess that you are already thinking, 'Hmm . . . If I want to be brilliant in that area, why aren't I doing that now?' The reason is that there are things holding you back. The next chapter explores what is holding you back. In it you'll find out how to replace some of those things with some more exciting powerful tools that will help you to achieve your vision in a tenth of the time that you thought would be possible.

Review

Doing a good job isn't good enough. You will get the rewards you deserve by doing a brilliant job, but brilliance doesn't happen by accident. You have to step up to the next level and focus on the areas where you want brilliance in your life right now.

Each of the stories in this chapter held a message, every one of the people who we have studied so far uses many of the techniques covered, but they all have one thing in common. They have . . .

brilliant
belief systems

What is it that's holding you back right now and what is it that drives you every day? This is what we shall explore in this chapter. If there was nothing holding you back, you'd be achieving your dreams right now; you'd already be doing the things that you really want to be doing. So there must be some things that hold us back.

You are about to learn how to eliminate the belief systems that are holding you back and replace them with something that is more exciting, more compelling. To do this you have to have enough compelling reasons why, enough reasons to make massive change, because making a slight shift is not going to make the difference you need.

Imagine that you have a CD playing in your head 24 hours a day, 7 days a week and this CD has been playing for years and years. All the things you feel about yourself, everything you know about yourself, are all embedded on to this CD that runs continuously in your head. We need to alter this CD during this part of the process otherwise it will hold you back, create obstacles and give you reasons why you shouldn't change. If you just take the CD out and adjust one or two tracks it's not going to be enough. We want to take out the old CD, scratch it and destroy it so much that you'll want to get rid of it. You'll never want to play it again.

Then you'll want to replace it, immediately, with a brand new set of beliefs – empowering, exciting and driving beliefs. Some of the beliefs may be ones that you already have. I'm not suggesting you get rid of

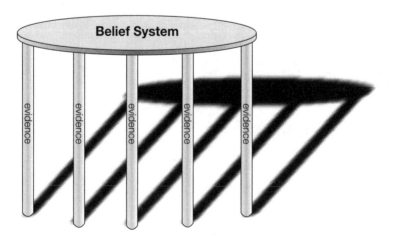

everything. There are parts of your life that are really fantastic; you want to hold on to those. You want to build on those parts. However, I think it would be safe to guess there are other parts of your life that you'd love to change right now!

What is a belief system anyway? What is something that we believe? How does it work? Here's a simple example used by lots of trainers to explain it. Imagine the table top is the belief system; it is something that you believe in, whatever it might be, it doesn't matter what it is – you believe it! The table top cannot stay there without the legs to support it. The legs are the evidence that supports the belief system.

'I **am** an absolutely incredible, wonderful, beautiful **person**.'

Say you had a belief system of, 'I am an absolutely incredible, wonderful, beautiful person.' Could you find the evidence to support it? I'm sure you could. There would be times when you would catch a look in the mirror and you'd say, 'Lookin' good.' You would get a compliment from somebody and you would hang on to that compliment. You would compare yourself with some other people and think, 'Wow! Compared to them I am an absolute superstar.' There is lots of evidence out there to support whatever belief system you might have.

You could also have a belief system that is, 'I'm an ugly pig and nobody likes me.' If you have that belief system, could you find a way to get the evidence to support that? Absolutely. Someone would make a comment about somebody else and you'd think they are talking about you! You look in the mirror, when you are not looking your best, and you say to yourself, 'Oh my God, that's what I look like!' You see other people who you believe look better than you and you say, 'If that's what I'm comparing myself to, no wonder I don't look so good.' You get a pimple and you think everyone is looking at it. You can create a belief system and find any evidence you wish to support it.

Here is another example: remember September 11, 2001? It was an extraordinary day that changed the world. I want you to go forwards to September 21, 10 days later, and ask yourself this question. Was today a good day to fly in America?

Some people have a belief system that says 'Yes, today was a great day to fly in America.' Other people have 'No, it was a terrible day to fly in America.' Which one is right? Well the truth is they are both right. And they will find different evidence to support their different viewpoints.

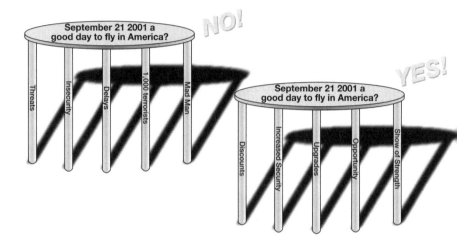

Take the belief system of the people who said 'No, it's not a good day to fly in America.' Why not? 'There are threats, delays. The newspapers say there are another thousand people out there who want to take over planes and do terrible things. It's a shocking time. That guy is a mad man and he'll do whatever it takes and the number one target right now is America.' This is the evidence you can find when you have the belief system of 'No'. You'll always find the evidence that you need to support your table top. Do you think the newspapers made a difference to the available evidence 10 days after that event? Do you think news programmes, television, radio and gossip created enough evidence to support the fact that September 21 is not a good day to fly in America? A huge amount of evidence was available to back up that point of view.

What if you had a belief system that was, 'Yes, today is a great day to fly in America.' Could you find the evidence? Of course – what about the increased security? It's never been a safer time to fly. Amazing discounts and upgrades are available. It's a show of strength. There's never been a better time to fly in America.

The reason I picked that date is because I had two phone calls, both from people in the United States; a friend of mine who is English and a friend of mine who is American. The first conversation was with the Chairman of a huge organization that we were organizing a conference for. The American Chairman of the company was flying over to the UK to speak to his top sales people based throughout Europe. We had the whole event organized: big video screens, awesome PA system, amazing lights, superb venue, all the details were perfect. There was only one thing missing, the Chairman of the company! And it was two days before the event. Then he called me to say, 'I won't be coming.'

•I can't believe this. Why not? Get on a plane and come over here now,• was my response.

•Well, I can't because it's not a very good time to fly, Michael.•

•No, it's a great time to fly. Get on a plane and come over here. Your top people from your organization want to meet you.•

•If they want to hear from me, can we do it by telephone?•

•Don't be crazy. You can't do it by telephone.•

•Can we do it by satellite? What if we paid for a satellite link, that would be cool?•

•No, you are getting on a plane and coming over here to meet your team. Now, that would be cool.•

Unfortunately he never did get on that plane. He ended up doing a telephone conversation to his top guys. How do you think they felt? That their leader could not get on a plane? Revising this edition I can tell you that he is no longer the Chairman of that company.

About five hours later I got another phone call from a friend of mine and she was giggling her head off at the other end of the telephone. I asked, 'Where are you now?'

'I'm in America and you'll not believe what's happened, Michael. Three days ago I realized that I had a few weeks when I wasn't going to be doing much work and I had £1,000 saved. I made a decision to see how far I could travel on £1,000. Then the craziest thing happened this morning. I was in Washington, in Dulles Airport, I had slept on a bench overnight, I went to the desk of one of the big airlines this morning at 6.00 o'clock and I said to them, "Do you have any flights down to Florida?" I wanted to get as close to Orlando as possible. She said, "Yes, we normally do eight flights a day but we're down to two at the moment." I replied, "Great, could you have a look and see if there's any availability? But before you do, I'm going to make this easy for you. I only have $50, will you fly me to Orlando?" Her response was along the lines of, "We're really sorry, we do have some great discounts available at the moment but we can't fly you for $50." '

My friend said, 'No problem at all,' turned around and started to walk towards the American Airlines desk who were waving people over, had big smiles and were doing anything at all to get business at that point. She had only taken three steps when a voice from behind the original desk shouted 'Excuse me, Miss, if you come back over here we're going to see what we can do.'

Here's the best bit. My friend confidently walked up to them and said, 'You have upset me, now you are going to have to upgrade me,' and sure enough they did! She flew Business Class from Washington to Orlando for $50 (including free champagne). When she arrived in Florida they were giving away free Disney tickets. Then she jumped aboard a free shuttle bus which took her to a Holiday Inn. She paid $20 a night to stay at the Holiday Inn. She went into Disney and as she walked through the gates they were so pleased to see her it was almost like, 'Quick, Mickey, put your head on. We have a guest!' There were no queues but the whole Disney atmosphere was there. It was incredible.

She finished her conversation by saying, 'Michael, there's never been a better time to fly in America.'

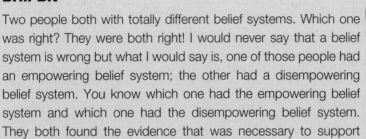

Take a look at what this really means. If you have a belief system, you'll find the evidence to support it. Let's go back to the areas where you said you wanted to be brilliant.

If you have a **belief system**, you'll find the **evidence to support it**.

Take the first one and then write down all the things that are holding you back from achieving that brilliance. Yes *all* the things that are holding you back. Everything! Write down things that you believe you can control and the things that you believe you can't. Take both of those areas and write everything down.

If you are reading this right now and thinking, 'Michael, I can only think of one or two things that are holding me back' then that's bull. Here are some clues:

Time	Debts
Money	Knowledge
Location	Qualifications
My boss	Being a woman
My partner	Being a man
Disability	Lack of transport
Being too fat	Fear of failure
Being too thin	Worrying about others
Lack of confidence	Illness
Lack of trust	Children
No support	Race
Laziness	Religion

There are so many things. If you're completely honest about *all* the things that hold you back, you'll be able to write quite a long list. Don't stop writing; just keep on going, keep that momentum, keep your physiology strong and just remember not to hold back at all. This is for you so write everything down, everything you can.

The **only way** of moving forward is **to be aware** of the things that are holding **you back**.

The only reason you should be continuing to read this chapter is because you have a full and complete list of things that are holding you back. You are probably thinking, 'Wait a minute. I thought this was going to be a positive, motivational book. I have written down all this stuff and it would depress me if I focused on it.' If so, good – that's exactly how it should feel. The good news is you are going to get rid of it.

The only way of moving forward is to be aware of the things that are holding you back. This awareness is going to make such a difference as we move to the next stage of the process. If you look down at your list, my guess is that as you look at some of the things that you wrote down you're thinking 'That's crazy. Why do I let that happen?' You could choose right now never to think about it again or to take those crazy actions. You could choose right now to change your belief system about it instantly and once you decide to change, you need never go back. You could do that right now with several things that are on that list, I am sure. Find them and tick them off your list. They are the easy ones.

Then there are others. When you look at them, you say, 'Wow, that's big stuff!' They are the real issues. They are the real big ones. So underline or put a star, draw circles around or do something that emphasizes they are key problems – big challenges. When you look at those you say, 'Yes, they really hold me back. They are the ones; I know they are the ones.' Identify those now.

Did you do it? I hope so. If you did, you should now have a real under-standing of what is holding you back from brilliance. Now look at those items and think, 'How would it feel if I could get rid of those things from my life – for ever?'

Already there's a part of your brain that is trying to be heard. It's a sneaky part of your brain, a part that introduces self-doubt. That part of your brain is probably saying, 'I can never change those things. It's just what life's like. Other people will think I'm crazy if I do that. Who on earth do I think I am?'

Just tell that part of your brain to shut up for a moment. It can have its time later when you have your new belief system in place!

The final part is very easy. When you look at your list, there will be one huge item. And when you look at that item, you think: 'Wow! That is just so big that I cannot go over it. It's so wide I can't go around it. It's so huge I can't go under it.' I call it the Rock. It's the number one thing that holds you back and we are going to get rid of it right now using . . .

6

brilliant
rock-busting

want you to identify what you truly believe is the Rock. Do it right now and mark it.

Guess which one we are going to start with? That's right, we're going to start with the big one, the Rock. It's no good fooling around just getting rid of little pebbles when we can go and do some big rock-busting. So we're going to get rid of the Rock right now.

You might have a Rock that somebody else would look at and say, 'That's crazy. What do you mean you are too young? What do you mean you are too old? What do you mean you haven't got the qualifications? What do you mean that you haven't got the right health? What do you mean that your family is holding you back? What do you mean that you don't have enough belief in what you do and fear failure? What do you mean you haven't got enough resources? What do you mean you haven't got enough money? Why on earth do you think you lack confidence?' They can't understand why you have that Rock and you probably can't understand theirs either. The only reason why it is real for you is because you have created the evidence to support that.

Here is what you are going to do. Just for fun, use your imagination. We're going to play around and see if we can create an affirmation; to create some words that, when used, would be the absolute total antithesis of what the Rock is, or what it means to you. This doesn't mean it's going to get rid of it; this is just a starting point. I'm really into practical methods. I love simple tools. I don't believe that if you just chant something for long enough that you are going to get rid of a problem. That's like going back to, 'no weeds, no weeds'. We don't want to just stand there and say, 'no Rock, no Rock'. That isn't going to get rid of the Rock.

I want you to start to create a different way of looking at the problem. The way we're going to do this is we're going to change the way that we think about this particular challenge and we're going to start by messing up the CD we mentioned at the start of this chapter. We're going to scratch the old CD and start to create some new data which is the absolute opposite of where we were before. Here are a few examples:

Lack of confidence

'I'm not a confident person.' You know when people say that, 'I'm not very confident; I'm shy,' they then automatically have that as a Rock. Of course if you *say* 'not confident', if you *say* 'shy', if you *act* shy and retiring, what type of results are you going to get? What type of evidence are you going to find? What if, instead, you created a new affirmation, a new belief system, one that is empowering? Something like, 'I have all the confidence that I need now.' You start to see and feel yourself being confident. Visualize yourself being outgoing, meeting people, smiling.

So rather than saying 'Oh, I'm not very confident,' tell yourself, 'I have all the confidence that I need now.'

Not enough time

'Oh, I haven't got the time'; 'There are not enough hours in the day'; 'You don't know everything I have to do.'

We all have the same amount of time. Some people just seem to manage it better than others. So what about instead of 'I haven't got the time' you say, 'I can find the time for everything that's important to me now.' Or simply: 'I can find the time.' You will start to see how the choice of words is so important; say it out loud, 'I can find the time for everything that is important to me now.' Great affirmation!

'I'm too old' or 'I'm too young'

Depending on how old you are, I'll give you a few different examples. What if your belief system was, 'I'm too old'. Could you instead say, 'My experience and wisdom puts me ahead of the game'? That is a great place to be, 'ahead of the game'. What if your belief system is, 'I'm too young' and you worry about not having enough experience? Could you instead say 'My innocence, my passion, my vibrancy will help me to achieve anything I put my mind to'? Is that more empowering than 'I'm too young'?

'I haven't got enough money'

Have you ever heard anybody say that one? That might be your Rock. You could be reading this now saying, 'That's my Rock, that's the one', 'I haven't got the money' or 'I haven't got the resources'. What if you were to say instead, 'All that I need is within me now!' Think about the earth as an abundant place. The earth *is* an abundant place and the abundance is coming towards you. Visualize your resources, the money or whatever it needs to be, coming towards you and tell yourself, 'All that I need is within me now.' Such an antithesis of 'I haven't got enough money'!

'I'm lazy' or 'I procrastinate'

Another classic, which we get a lot of people saying on our business and personal development programmes, 'I'm just lazy', 'I just procrastinate', 'I should do more', 'I should do this. I should do that.' I heard a story about 'should' once. 'When people say I *should* do this, I *should* do that, you know what's going to happen? They're going to *should* all over themselves! You have got to make it a must.' So instead of saying 'I'm lazy', you could say, 'I have the enthusiasm, drive and energy to achieve anything that I put my mind to. I make it a must!'

Brill Bit

As you start to use different language, you take different actions. This isn't 'airy fairy' stuff; it isn't flowery language for the sake of it. This is you starting to re-program your nervous system, reprogramming the way that you think by changing your choice of words. And best of all you will start to get immediate, noticeably different results.

However, words are not enough. At the end of the day, it all comes down to the actions that we take. Actions are the most important thing. As you play around with the words, don't say them in your head, say them out loud. The physiology of speaking out loud will make this stick and when you find the right words, when you have played with those words, looked at the right adjectives, listened for the right tonality – when you have really thought about it, say it out loud again and again so it becomes part of you.

Words are **not enough**.

At the end of the day,

it all comes down to

the actions that we take.

You want this to be something that you will say on a frequent basis. So even if that old Rock starts to sneak back later after you have eliminated it – if you get a small seed of doubt – you can come right back with your new affirmation.

Here are two more techniques for eliminating the Rock, but not just the Rock, all those other limiting beliefs you listed before. We start with the Rock because once you have removed the Rock, you can get rid of other limiting beliefs very easily. You are going to eliminate limiting belief systems one by one. Some of them are going to be blasted out of the water, others are going to take a little bit more effort.

The first technique we will use is very practical. The second one is much more intuitive, about the way that you think about a process, about using a part of your brain that you may not access too often.

Circles of Influence versus Circles of Concern

The first area is called, 'Circles of Influence versus Circles of Concern', adapted from Dr Stephen Covey. This is a method that relies on you sitting down, putting pen to paper, developing techniques and looking at clear strategies. Look at the diagram; you'll notice that there are two circles. The big circle is the Circle of Concern. This circle is the one that has all the problems, all the concerns, all the worries, all the things that are holding you back. It truly is a Circle of Concern. The great thing about the Circle of Concern, even though it is there and it is very real, is you don't have to do anything about it! All you have to do is be concerned about those things; you don't have to take any actions. You can moan and groan about it all day, but it doesn't matter. You don't have to take any actions! I'm sure you'll know some people who love to spend all of

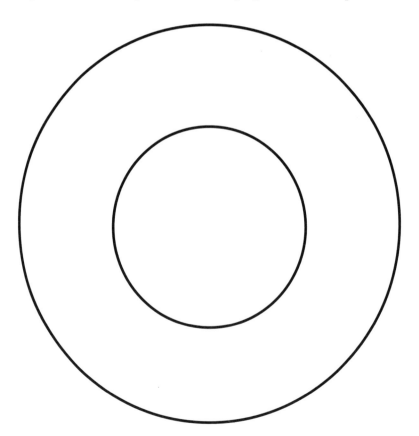

their time in their Circle of Concern. In fact, the more time they can spend in their Circle of Concern the better, because it's a great place to be. Why? Because it's comfortable. Also, people give you sympathy when you are in your Circle of Concern. They understand you have problems. They feel sorry for you. And you feel nice hanging on to that problem. But you won't be able to move on to the next level if you do that, so it's time to get rid of it now.

Here's what we do. Use the Circle of Concern and fill in as many concerns around your 'Rock' as you can. List all the things that are holding you back: what other people say, how you feel about it, the results, the actions, the problems, everything. Put it all in to the Circle of Concern. Go on, see if you can fill the whole of that big fat circle with concerns, even if it looks like a mad ramble on the paper, just keep writing all the things, all the concerns, write as many as you can. Do the exercise right now.

Now you have a circle full of concerns. So what are you going to do about it? If you were to continuously focus on the Circle of Concern, then the smaller circle, the Circle of Influence, would start to get smaller and smaller until eventually the Circle of Influence (what you can truly do about your situation) would have shrunk down so far it really would feel like, 'There is nothing I can do.'

Before it has a chance to do that, let's change your focus. Just think of one thing, one key thing, to put into your Circle of Influence. A specific idea, that when you write it *and take action*, it will make some difference to eliminating the Rock. It doesn't matter how small it is, it doesn't matter how spectacular it is, just think of one idea and write it in your Circle of Influence. One idea, one thing that you can do in your Circle of Influence that will make a difference. Do it now.

If you wrote, 'Change my attitude', 'Find some time' or something vague like that, then as your coach I'm going to give you a 'Must try harder'! Get specific about what you're going to do. If you have Lack of Confidence as your Rock and you wrote, 'Try to be more confident', then not a great deal will change. If you want to be brilliant at change, you need to take clear and specific actions. Something like 'Read five books on building confidence.' Then find five ideas from each book that you can apply, measure the difference they make and then focus on mastering those ideas.

Or if you had something about not having enough qualifications and you wrote, 'Get some qualifications', then again this is too vague. Instead go for something like, 'Prepare a list of all the qualifications I need by asking key influencers what they think I should have. Get a list of all the courses available in my area and find the one that is most suited to me. Meet with the tutors and decide if this is the right route for me to take.' Can you see how much more powerful that type of action is?

Once you have thought of one thing, you might be able to think of two things or even three things. At that point stop. Only ever have a maximum of three actions in your Circle of Influence.

When we start to crack that Rock we can start to make smaller stones, those stones become tiny stones, those tiny stones become pebbles, and those pebbles become sand and then we can just wash it away.

The three rules to remember when completing your Circles of Influence and Circles of Concern are:

1 Always acknowledge the concerns before you move on to what you can influence.

2 Only have three positive actions in your Circle of Influence, never more.

3 Always make the actions entered in the Circle of Influence clear, positive and specific.

Brilliant! I don't know if you have realized, but you've already started on your plan. Take a look at where you were a few chapters ago. Before Chapter 3 you were probably unaware of what was really important, and what you wanted to be brilliant at. Remember, you made a decision about what you wanted to be brilliant at and you recognized there are things that are holding you back. Very few people ever go through this process, very few people have actually sat down and really thought about what was holding them back. Then you took an opportunity to identify those different areas; many, many different areas, and really got focused. You then identified the ones that were causing the biggest challenges of all.

From there, in this chapter, you moved to the next stage and acknowledged the big one, the Rock, the one that, if you could get rid of it, would make such a huge difference. Then you attacked the challenge by exploring a different way to look at the situation. You started to create a new belief system. You didn't have much evidence but all we wanted to do was to choose new words, choose a new affirmation.

The next stage is amazing because you really focused using your Circle of Influence and Circle of Concern. You decided that you don't want to spend another moment focusing on those concerns because your focus is now going to be on those one, two or three things in your Circle of Influence, the ones that are going to make a difference. As you do this, you'll start to see your Circle of Influence getting bigger, and the bigger it gets, the stronger it becomes. And the more you'll feel yourself becoming confident about tackling the challenges.

I guarantee that any challenges will become less and less significant in your life and the new belief system, the new one that you are creating right now, will start to take over.

I want to give you more tools further on in this book for creating a vision, for finding people who can help you, to look at ways you can raise your game, to understand how you can change your physiology, how you can mentally rehearse. But take a moment to reflect as this is an important moment – you've started the process of being brilliant now!

Brill Bit

Understanding that brilliance doesn't happen by accident and that brilliant people have a range of tools to move forward in a number of different ways is a fundamental part of the process. Brilliance is within your grasp!

Brilliant intuition

This is a much deeper, more intuitive way to tackle a particular problem and it's called, 'Using a Mastermind Group'. Your intuition is the most incredible, amazing thing that you have. The answer to so many problems, the answer to so many challenges, the answer to so many questions is there in your intuition right now.

How do we develop our intuition so that we can tap into it whenever we need to? I remember reading one of the very first personal development books ever written; it was called, *Think and Grow Rich* by Napoleon Hill. Napoleon Hill was absolutely inspirational. He found the most successful people on the planet and studied what it was that made them so successful. He interviewed 500 people over a period of 20 years. He met with Presidents, he consulted the leaders of industry, interrogated leaders of communities, and found that they all had certain things in common. The characteristics we explored in Chapter 2 were all there but also many of these successful people had a group of people whom Hill referred to as a 'Mastermind Group'. This was a group of people with whom they could sit down and who would give them great advice.

Wouldn't it be fantastic to surround yourself with amazing people whom you could ask for advice? Well you can. There is a superb technique, a wonderful tool that you can use if you ever need advice from somebody and it's just a few magic words. If you don't get anything else out of this chapter other than using these magic words, it will make a big difference in your life. The magic words are, 'I need your help.' Humans have a natural way of responding when somebody says, 'I need your help.' If you call somebody, or if you meet up with them and say, 'I need your help,' from most people the response is going to be, 'What can I do?'

The magic words are:

Find a mentor (or two)

One of the keys on how to be brilliant is to find mentors who will push you, advise you, coach and encourage you. Mentors are better than you! Asking a mate if he or she will be a mentor in most cases won't help. Asking a person who is the best you know in your field, sport, hobby, interest, industry, etc. is a far more effective way of getting results.

Meet with your mentors regularly and keep them informed of your progress. If you have chosen well, your mentors will be very successful and probably very busy. Don't let them down.

Your mentors will be able to introduce you to people who will make things happen faster and bigger. Treat your mentors with respect. One day you will be able to do something for them. Take this opportunity and make it happen quickly.

Brill Bit

The first time you meet your mentor formally, take them a gift. Make it personal and imaginative. If possible, write a message on it; if not, attach a card with a message neatly written inside. Your mentor will be grateful, but more importantly they will show others and the contacts will flow.

What if you can't physically meet the group of people who will help you to achieve what you want to achieve? That's when your intuition is going to come into place to use the power of visualization. Visualization is amazing because there are no limits to it. If you can visualize it, then it just seems to happen.

Which is the biggest nation in the world? Not China, not America. The biggest nation in the world is your imagination. Corny, I know, but you'll be using it!

If you could have Winston Churchill as an advisor or mentor would you accept him? What about Richard Branson or Billy Connolly? Using your imagination, you can.

You can create your own 'Mastermind Group' just as Napoleon Hill discovered. It's just you won't have the people physically with you, but you will have them mentally.

Imagine you are sitting in a very comfortable place and there are some spaces around a table and those spaces are to be filled with people that you know would give you great advice. Here's the secret – you need never have met them. They can be people from history. They can be people whom you admire. They can be people whom you have read about. Just start and imagine each of those places being filled with a person who can give you great advice. Stop reading for a moment, take a few minutes to create your Mastermind Group, then mentally have a conversation with those people and ask them for advice. Let your mind go for it here, really explore the views of your Mastermind Group.

How did you find that? Sometimes when I have done this with people on our programmes I have spent a lot of time getting people very relaxed going through the process and at the end of it they have said, 'Well it was OK, but ... These are the people I had in my head – Gandhi, Billy Connolly, the Queen and a friend of mine from school. I sat them down, people I knew I could get great advice from, and I felt like I was making up the conversation. I had to make up their conversation for them! And I had to think about the type of thing that they would say.'

'Ah Ha!' I always say, 'That's exactly how it should feel. If it feels like you are making up the conversation and it feels like you are making up the things that they would say, guess what you're doing, you are using your what? Your intuition!'

This tool for using your intuition, the Mastermind Group, is just a tool for tapping into things that you already know.

Here's something interesting about intuition – your intuition will always be right. It will always be right even if you think it's wrong. What do I mean by that? Sometimes your intuition will tell you something and you'll get a message but you won't quite understand *why* you've got that particular message. What tends to happen next is that, suddenly something jumps out and you say, 'Yes, that's what it meant! Now I get it!'.

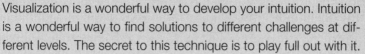

Brill Bit

Visualization is a wonderful way to develop your intuition. Intuition is a wonderful way to find solutions to different challenges at different levels. The secret to this technique is to play full out with it.

Getting real

If you sit down, say 'OK, I'm going to close my eyes now and then I'm going to picture Richard Branson.' In your visualization you then say, 'Hi Richard, how do I make a lot of money?' Branson replies 'Work hard!' You open your eyes and say, 'That didn't work.' If you think like that, guess what's going to happen? You're not going to get the results that you want. But if you really said, 'Yes, I'm going to go for this. I'm going to sit down. I'm going to intuitively think about the right people around me,' and 'Yes, one of those people may be Richard Branson for business advice.' Or you may choose somebody else and say, 'I'm going to ask lots of questions and go with the flow.' You'll get amazing responses. You may choose to have somebody for relationship advice. You may choose somebody from your past who has always been there and given you great counsel before. When you sit down with those people in your imagination, really feel what it is they're saying.

Once you get the advice, take massive action and you know what's going to happen to that Rock, don't you? You're now taking dynamite to it! There's no longer a little crack there; you're starting to blow it to pieces. It doesn't have to stop there, not just with the Rock. You can use your intuition for so many different areas of your life, develop it, learn from it, grow with it, but above all, trust it.

Once the Rocks begin to disappear and confidence grows, I have often found people believe they are liberated. Then as quickly as they found success, they begin to lose it. Their life seems to go out of balance and they find that even with the success, they haven't found happiness. Don't worry, this won't happen to you. You will be successful, brilliant and happy. How do I know? Because you'll have . . .

7

brilliant
values

What is a value? People immediately associate values with a way you might feel, things that you would do, your actions, or your belief systems. I believe that values are the most important, integral part of your quality of life. Truly, if you have the right values, and the right beliefs to go with those values, then your quality of life can improve beyond anything you could have imagined.

Sir John Templeton became one of the most successful investors of all time and a billionaire in the process. His deep-rooted values meant he would not be swayed to move from his core beliefs. He would save and invest 50 per cent of his income (a value and habit he developed before he became a professional investor) and he would give millions of dollars to worthy causes every year as well as supporting numerous individuals and projects. He has written many books about the significance of a spiritual life and the importance of giving.

Nicholas van Hoogstraten also acquired massive wealth by investing in property. His values were based on greed and hatred for the people who paid his rents. After a long history of fighting with his neighbours and business associates, he was eventually found guilty of manslaughter and sentenced to 10 years in prison. He too would not be swayed from his values.

What type of wealthy person would you like to be? In the case of the people mentioned, money simply magnified their values.

Values are right up there with oxygen!

As we go through this chapter, there may be times when you think, 'Where are we going here?' or 'What do you want me to achieve from this?' At this point it is important that you stick with the chapter. When I ask you to do an exercise, complete it thoroughly before moving on to the next stage. This is an important foundation on which you'll build your brilliant future.

I want to start off by asking you an important question, 'What is your question?' What is your life question? What question do you find yourself asking more than any other throughout the day? Most people have never stopped to consider what is the question we ask ourselves again and again. You could be saying, 'Michael, I don't have a question that I ask again and again. I don't have a question that pops up into my head every few moments.' When I give you some examples of other people's life questions, then you may start to get an idea of what it is that you are asking yourself.

‘**What** is your question?’

You are not to judge this question; I just want you to be aware of the question that's in your head. Here's a list of some of the questions that other people may ask themselves.

How can I be part of this?

What can I do to make this better?

Will I ever find somebody who will love me?

Why does nobody like me?

Why do I get dissatisfied with everything I do?

Why can't I see things through?

What's for dinner?

Why am I here?

What is the point?

Why am I unhappy?

What's next?

Some of those questions are very empowering and others are very dis-empowering. Even some of the ones that on the surface may seem to be an empowering question, when you start to dig really deep down, ask yourself, 'What are the consequences of asking this question all the time?'

I used to have a question that I found myself asking again and again. 'How can I be part of this?' In other words, I was asking, 'What's happening and am I in on it?' At first that seemed like a great question because it opened up many opportunities. When something came along I would want to be part of it. I knew that I could find exciting new avenues, different ways to develop my life by being part of various different groups and by getting involved with countless different ideas and projects. However, I also realized, by doing this I wasn't able to stay focused on the most important things in my life. So rather than having a conversation with somebody and being totally focused on helping them to communicate, helping them to express what they wanted to do, I was more interested in the conversation that was taking place behind them. I was wondering what was happening, and should I be involved with this one? I realized that this question was actually disempowering me. I changed my question.

To change my question, I spent time working on what was important to me, the skills I had and the energy I possessed. My new question was 'How can I use my unstoppable energy to stay focused on my life's mission?'

As soon as I got this new question into my mind I started to become more and more focused. Many opportunities would come along but, by continually asking that question, I realized that I could stay focused on the most important things. I made better choices, I wrote this book! I made better decisions and, most importantly, I didn't feel like I was missing out if I wasn't involved in everything!

So back to the question, 'What is your life's question?' What's the question that you ask more than any other? A great way to look at this is to think, 'When I wake up each morning what am I saying to myself? When I travel to go to work or to do my daily tasks, what question am I asking myself? As I move through my life, what question am I asking myself again and again?'

At this point don't worry too much if it doesn't leap to mind. What I would like you to do is to become aware that there is a question. It may be that long after you've read this book, the question will suddenly pop into your head.

When you have your life's question, ask the key most important question: *Is this question an empowering question or a disempowering question?* If it's an empowering question, great. Keep asking it or even improve on it. Intensify and ask that question more often. If it is a disempowering question, or it doesn't serve you, or doesn't take you to the place where you really want to get to, then think about changing it to a new question. Then ask yourself that new question consciously throughout your day. Soon it will become part of your subconscious and that means it's a part of you.

Now let's focus on values and start to think about your values right now. In this section you're going to look at whether they're the right values for you. Then you are going to explore whether you may want to change those values and how you can make them a key part of your life by creating new rules to support them.

Let's make it easy. First the guidelines. You must be totally honest as you go through this process because, if you don't, you will find that you are kidding yourself and shortly afterwards you will realize that those values are not the most important ones to you. It's like going to a slimming club. You can tell yourself you are doing well, but the evidence will be seen at the weekly weigh-in. If you are doing this process with somebody else, it's likely that your values will be different from that person's. Remember, they are your values; there's no right or wrong answer. It's about what's important to you and about where you ultimately want to go in your life.

So let's start by asking the question: what are your current values? Not what you would *like* them to be, but what your current values are right now. How do you live your life? Let me give you an idea about different things you might consider to be a value.

- **Success:** Do you want to be successful? Do you want to lead the field? Do you want to be number one?
- **Fun:** Do you have fun as one of your values? Do you want to laugh and enjoy life to the absolute full?
- **Passion:** Is that something that you are excited about? Do you really want to experience huge passion in everything you do, so you'll go the extra mile and do whatever it takes?
- **Greed:** Could you have greed as a value? Absolutely. If you think,

'Yes, I want more, more, more, more' then you can have greed as a value.

- **Enthusiasm:** Do you leap out of bed, and run through your day with so much enthusiasm that you are going to knock the socks off people?

- **Power:** Is power important to you? Do you want to lead in a way that people look at you and they say, 'That person is powerful; that person has gone beyond success. They bring in power'?

- **Love:** Is love one of your values? To love other people and to be loved. How do you feel about love?

- **Integrity/honesty:** Do you believe that truth is high on your list of values? Do you tell it how it is even if there are consequences? Do you feel mortally wounded when others betray this value?

- **Recognition:** Is that an important value for you? Do you want to be recognized for the work that you have done? Do you want to be recognized for the contribution that you make? Do you want to be recognized for who, where and, most importantly, what you are doing? Then that would be recognition.

- **Rejection:** You may wonder how on earth you could have rejection as a value, but some people do, because that is an important part of their lives. They worry about it. It's right at the forefront. Something they would think about every single day. When it is that prevalent, then it is a value.

- **Control:** Is that a value for you? Do you want to be in control? Do you want to know exactly what's happening? Control is important to you and you know the direction that you want to go in. You know exactly what's going to be happening, so you want to be able to control that in every single possible way. You are a hands-on sort of a person.

- **Blame:** Do you find yourself blaming others for situations that occur around you? Do you want to know who is causing the problems so you can 'get to the bottom of it'?

- **Excitement:** Are you the type of person who jumps off cliffs with a hang-glider (or without one!)? Do you love to go on expeditions, or really want to take risks and go for it in an exciting way? Or do you look for excitement within the work that you do? Do you think that excitement is vital within relationships? What do you think about excitement and could that be one of your values?

- **Security:** The antithesis of excitement. Do you want to be secure? Do you want to know exactly where everything is going to be on a regular basis? Do you want to come home and know that certain things are going to be in a certain place? Do you love that feeling of total security?

- **Worry:** Do you find yourself worrying all the time? Making it a habit to see things to be concerned about? Believing that your worry is a way of showing that you care?

- **Contribution:** Do you believe that contribution is critical? Do you want to give your time and resources to help others without any recognition? Are you the first to volunteer – even for the nasty jobs?

- **Health:** Are you focused on your health? Do you watch carefully what you eat, focusing on really taking care of yourself, believing that nourishment and vitality are the key to the quality of life?

- **Creativity:** Do you look to be creative in all that you do? Are you constantly thinking of new ways to do things? Do you believe it is important to think out of the box and move the boundaries? Do you love to see the results of your creative activities?

There are many different types of values. I would like you to stop reading for a moment and write down what you believe are your values. You can write down as many or as few as you like. Think carefully for a moment about what are your current values. Not what you would *like* them to be, this is what your current values are right now. Be totally honest and start writing.

Did you take the time to write down your values? I hope you did because this is one of the most important areas of this whole book. You are about to find out why. To do this successfully you must follow the instructions carefully and really play full out with me. If you didn't do it, stop reading and do it right now. Maybe you have started to think of other extra values that you can add to your list. That's fine – keep adding to the list. You may not like the descriptions that I gave earlier for some of those other values. Remember, the values written earlier in the prevous pages are not necessarily yours; they were just examples. So any word, any descriptions you use are entirely up to you.

The next thing I'd like you to do is to put them in an order of importance. Go through your list asking, 'Which is the most important value that I have on that list *now?*' Not which one would I like it to be. When you have decided which one it's going to be, write the number 1 next to that value. Then identify the second most important, that doesn't mean that when you write number 2 that value isn't as important; it just means that you are being very critical. You are looking at things in detail to decide the order they go in. This is your Value List as it is right now, so just rank them 1 through to 5, 1 through to 10, however many values you might have. Do this now.

I hope you've done that. At this moment in time, you should have a list of values, and have them in an order starting with number 1 and going through to however many values you may have.

Brill Bit

How many people do you know who have ever consciously thought about their values, bothered to write them down and put them in order? You have!

Here's another important question. What type of person do you ultimately want to become? Think carefully about this for a moment. It's not a question that we ask ourselves very often. Now very specifically, write down a description of the type of person you would ultimately want to become. As before, stop and do it now.

So now that you've decided the type of person you ultimately want to become and written it down, I have one more question. Look at your list of current values and ask, 'Do these values, in this order, allow me to achieve my ultimate destiny?' Think very carefully about this for a moment. 'Do *these values*, in *this order* allow me to *achieve* my ultimate destiny?'

'Do these values, in this order allow me to achieve my ultimate destiny?'

Why is this so important? It's simple. If your values are incongruent with the type of person you ultimately want to become, then it will be impossible for you to achieve that particular destiny.

I often work with people who say how much they would love to be known as a person who gives beyond anything they could imagine, who contributes massively to society, who is able to grow, to love and to cherish their families and their family lives, to care for the people around them and to give so much. Then they look back at their list and see that values 1, 2 and 3 are power, recognition and risk. Do these values in this order allow them to achieve their ultimate destiny? Of course they don't.

About 95 per cent of people sit down and realize that one of the reasons they are not achieving their ultimate destiny – why they are not truly satisfied with their lives – is because their value system is either completely wrong, some part of the list is wrong, or the values are in the wrong order. They look at their value system and they understand for the first time that their values in their current order will not allow them to achieve their ultimate destiny.

This is an exciting time. Yes, you may have found something that is wrong but now you know exactly where you are in your life and can replace, change and tweak. You can also add new rules which are going to help you to achieve your ultimate destiny fast!

Just think, right now you're at a moment in time when, if you understand exactly what is happening now, your life will never be the same again. I don't know about you, but I'm excited as I write this; I hope you share that excitement as you read it! Some people may be thinking 'OK, I'll redo my values later.' Don't do it later; do it right now! Life will change for you right now by taking the correct actions in the next few moments.

Life **will change** for you right now by taking the **correct actions** in the next few moments.

Whether you need to change, replace or just tweak your values, here's stage 1 of creating a new value system for yourself. Ask yourself this: in order to become the type of person that I ultimately want to become, what type of values would a person like that have? Just focus now on that person. What type of values would they have? I'm going to ask you to write these values down, really explore this, almost like a brainstorm. Then choose your words very carefully, because these words are going to be very empowering to you. These words are going to be ones that you will use to shape your destiny. These words are going to be the ones that will get you up in the morning and will help you to make decisions throughout your life. Every single day these words will come into your mind. Take time now to imagine the type of person you ultimately want to become and what that person's values would be.

The next stage is exactly as we did before. Go through your list, decide if they are truly the values that you really want to have in order to become that person who you ultimately want to become. Once you have chosen the ones that are most important, put them in order 1 to 5, 1 to 10, 1 to 3, however many you may have. Then ask yourself the question: 'Do these values in this order allow me to achieve my ultimate destiny?' When you look at your new list and think about the question, can you say 'Yes' from your heart? If you can answer 'Yes' with a passion and a total certainty, then you know that this value list is the thing that's going to drive you towards your destiny. Congratulations, you have made some amazing progress.

What if you look at that list and you say, 'Yeah, they are OK'? In this case your values are not coming from a place of passion and certainty and from your heart. Dig deep down, dig really deep and ask yourself, truly now, truly, 'Do those values, in this order, allow me to achieve my ultimate destiny?' If the answer is 'No', then get back to work and do them again.

Right now you have a list. We call these your Moving Towards Values. Your Moving Towards Values are very important, but remember, I did say we wanted to make it as easy as possible. We wanted to make it easy to live those values.

Take a step back for a moment and think about how you created your value system in the first place. Before you were able to write down values, how do they become values to you? They only become values, true values, if you live them, if you live them every single day. Think about how you create a value in the first place. You decide what is important to you, then you create a belief system to support that, then you find the evidence to support that belief system. They are the rules. Who made the rules? Think about it. Who made rules to give you the values that you used to have? That order you wrote down. Who made up the rules?

You did!

If one of your values was recognition, there's probably a time you could go back to in your life when recognition was not there. A time came along when recognition was important and you thought, 'Yeah, I feel good about this. I want to be recognized for what I do.' You made it important. You also decided what the rules were going to be. Your rules for recognition may be that you want to have something written down in a letter from somebody, in a card saying what a great job you've done. Somebody else might have recognition as one of their values and all they need is a kind word from somebody. Somebody else may have recognition and all it needs is an appreciative look. We create the rules. We create the rules that fit the belief system. The belief system forms the value.

Take a look at the new list you have. Let's think about the *new rules* that you are going to create to help you to live those new values every single day. Here's a tip: make it easy for yourself! Why do you want to make it easy? Simple, why make it hard?

Let's take the value of fun. Your first rule could be, I have fun every time I hear laughter. Notice it's not every time I laugh. Every time I hear laughter allows you to experience the value of fun more often. Remember, you make the rules.

If you should decide, I'm going to feel fun every time it starts to rain, you can. Imagine how much fun you can have with that! Imagine that you decide to feel the value of fun every time you see a bright colour or that you could choose to have fun just by doing one single action.

Perhaps a final example here could be the value of success. How do you measure success? For some people the rules are simple. When I'm number one, when I'm absolutely certain that I've done every single thing that I could ever do to achieve every bit of success in my life, that's when I'm going to feel the value of success. When my salary hits a certain point, that's when I'll know I've been successful. When I'm driving a certain car, that's how I'll know I've been successful. I'm successful when I'm getting so many sales. When my kids tell me I've done this, when my friends recognize me for doing something else, that's when I'll feel successful.

That's great. But when will they ever truly feel success? They will probably never feel true success because they are always pushing themselves to the next level. This is great in terms of goals, but remember, we want to live these values, we want to feel these values, every day. Could you say instead:

- I feel success every time I turn up somewhere on time?
- I feel success every time I get to the end of the day and I have connected with other people and made them happy.
- I feel success every time that I feel certain about any project I am working on in my life.
- I feel success every time I see my kids smile because I created them.
- I feel success every time I look out in the world and see other people being successful.

Create that as a rule and you will feel success every day, and become more successful day by day because you changed the value system and you changed the rules.

The next exercise is one that could be easier for some people. What I would like you to do is stop reading and really concentrate on the rules that you're going to create. These are the rules to support your new value system. They will allow you to become the type of person you would ultimately want to become. So stop reading and do it now.

Congratulations! You have done something that very few people ever take an opportunity to do in their lives. You have created a new value system. You have created rules to fit with that value system. The next stage is to live that value system. Writing it down is an exciting process. Living it is the most exciting thing you could ever choose to do.

Brill Bit

Create a visual image of your new value system and the new rules. Make sure you look at it every single day. Fill your mind with these values. Work on them. Adjust them. Change them if you need to, and ask yourself questions about the type of person that you would ultimately want to become.

I know for many people this is the most exciting part of this book. It can be challenging to understand. You may need to read this chapter several times to get a deep understanding. Please work hard and endeavour to create a value system that will empower you. Your life will never ever be the same again.

So far we have focused the brilliance message on you. But let me ask you a question. Do you at any point in your life have to work with or spend time with other human beings? Thought so. Well in order for you to be the very best in these situations you have to know how to create . . .

brilliant
teams

You must have heard it a million times: TEAM – **T**ogether **E**veryone **A**chieves **M**ore. I'm sure they do but let's get a little selfish for a moment and think how brilliant teams may benefit you.

Why do it all yourself when you can work with other brilliant people to get the job done in half the time? Ah, the other brilliant people. That could be the problem. So let's start by taking a look at how you put together your brilliant team. The same rules apply in any area. Some of the stuff works all of the time; all of the stuff works some of the time – you choose.

Can you remember a time when you have been part of a brilliant team? Was it during school or in your first job? Was it a community project or a drama production? Perhaps it was a sports team or a special workforce. We have all had great experiences of brilliant teams. Now you can take away the luck and create brilliant teams whenever you need them.

And guess what? You can build a team. Complete a project. Learn from the project. Dismantle the team. Improve your teamwork and have a whole lot of fun in just 90 days.

Selecting the perfect team

Have you ever heard this one? Choose people in a team who don't really get on, they will stretch each other. Who comes up with this stuff? Choose people who may give different opinions, but don't choose people you don't like! Think about a time when a person whom you have really admired, rated as good or better than you, respected or loved has given a different opinion. Now think about a person whom you don't really like, who rubs you up the wrong way, who has different values from your own and imagine them giving you a different opinion. Now choose who you want on your team. Incidentally, you'd still feel the same way about them even if they agreed with you! *The trick is to find people who complement each other but who get on.*

Think of a soccer team; 11 goal keepers might share skill sets but it would be a terrible team. What about an amazingly skilful goalkeeper who has had a personal challenge with the equally talented defenders. They don't communicate and what happens? LOSERS!

So here's a thought. Write down the characteristics you'd like to see in a perfect team. If you are putting together a team for you, this will be an exciting thing to do because you'll also be able to develop your team along these criteria. If you are a member of a team, or going to be a member of a team, still do it!

Brill Bit

If you are putting together a team at work, write 'ads' for the type of people you are looking for in the same style you would see in the newspaper recruitment pages. Leave the ads on people's desks. One may look a little like this:

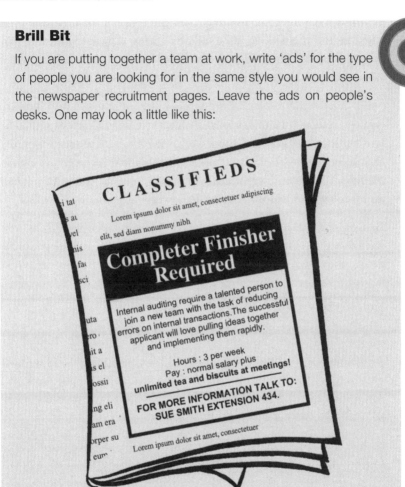

So now let's assume you have recruited your brilliant team. Give them some oomph! I'm going to focus on the workplace for this section, but these rules are transferable.

How many times have you sat down in a meeting with a new team and the leader has started with a dull, dull, dull ramble about what you are going to do? Test this out.

Make a bold statement about this new team using key words to describe how you want it to be: outstanding, best, imaginative, funky, fun, rapid, etc. Then ask who would like to be part of a team like this? Anyone who says 'no', ask them for an alternative or suggest they move to a different team! Your leadership will be measured as much by your inability to get rid of poor performers as it will be for recruiting good ones!

Spend a few minutes developing a set of rules and make sure they are neatly typed up. One set is printed on dayglo paper and laminated (to take to every meeting) and the others are passed out. It all sounds very practical so far and with these little tips, you should start to create a good team that consistently produces poor results. Join the rest of the planet! So what needs to happen to make a team brilliant?

Here are the five steps to making any team brilliant. And just in case you were thinking, 'I'm not a team leader, I can't do that', change your language, become a leader, and step up to brilliance – the rest will soon follow!

1 Total immersion and mastery

Total immersion is the very best way to learn anything. I had a friend who went to driving lessons for an hour every week for three years and didn't pass her test until she'd been on a one-week intensive driving course. At the end of the week she passed her test.

Look at the stats, even with cancellations, bad weather and holidays she had 40 lessons per year = 120 hours over 3 years and failed three times. On her intensive course she drove for a maximum of 25 hours but passed first time.

Mastery comes when you truly understand your subject. Imagine a team of five people who are all committed to mastering their project or task. How would it feel to be held to a higher level by those around you? Mastery sets that standard.

2 Know your outcome

How will you know when you've been successful? More teams start on projects with clear outcomes than ever before. Meetings take hours, reporting is slow, and worst of all you don't know if you've been successful.

By defining clear outcomes early on, you know your target. Actually that's what fantastic teams do. Brilliant teams create great language around those outcomes. They tell others their plans to be accountable, and write them down as goals using the three P's to ensure they are driven towards achieving their goal.

3 Focus

Where your focus goes, energy flows. Dave Charleton is the Chief Executive and Chairman of the highly successful Officers Club clothing stores. I was interviewing him recently about his success and we came onto the subject of teams. He said, 'When teams are focused they are brilliant, they have to be.' He gave me the example of the after effect of when he did a brilliant deal to buy 65 stores from a division of C&A.

'We had 10 weeks to close, refurbish, recruit, train, stock and launch 65 shops. The team were brilliant, focusing on using all of their skills to complete the project on time and on budget.' Looking back he was amazed they did it, but at the time everyone knew that a total focus was required.

What do you think the consequences would have been if they had people on the team who were not focused?

4 Pace – West Wing teams!

The popular American drama series *The West Wing* gave a glimpse of what it's like to run the USA from the famous West Wing of the White House. In each episode President Bartlett, brilliantly played by Martin Sheen, runs an amazing team of advisors, experts, directors and assistants who make rapid decisions and carry out plans with brutal pace.

Even though it's 'just TV', I brought the same ideas into my organization with amazing results. I've been raving about West Wing speed, West Wing teams and West Wing meetings ever since!

West Wing speed means you accelerate everything you do by 50 per cent. Yes 50 per cent! But you must do it in the context of the team. The key is to get everyone moving at the same speed from the moment they come into the workplace until they go home. You don't have to be the manager to do this (in many ways it's better if you aren't), but you must keep up the momentum.

West Wing teams rely on the fact that the team is always right, even when you're wrong! Let me explain. The team can dissect, criticize, admit defeat, moan and groan all they like but to the outside world you are always one unit, defending every action and making the most out of every situation. Politics at the highest level can be tumbled by the smallest crack. So can your team!

West Wing meetings are my favourite. Let me begin by telling you what they *don't* do when having a team meeting in *The West Wing*. They don't:

- Arrive 10 minutes late.
- Dawdle into the room.
- Start the meeting by finding out 'who wants tea and who wants coffee'.
- Chat about what they did at the weekend.
- Set up a Power Point presentation.
- Apologize for not having enough copies of the 28-page report.
- Tap a teacup to get attention.
- Spend the first 5 minutes deciding who will take notes.
- Ever say 'we'll park it 'til next week'.
- Say 'Look at the time we've been in here for hours, should we send out for sandwiches because Terry hasn't started his presentation yet and Sue still needs to bottom out our policy on the new strategy for Q3? But we'll have to move rooms because Gavin and his team of 30 need this room at 12.00 to do an analysis on VAT implications on expenses during the Q2. So let's take a vote on who wants to move rooms or who wants to put off the presentation from Terry and Sue's agenda

item until next week. But before we do that, can I just have a quick indication again, who wants tea and who wants coffee . . . ?'

The West Wing team meetings are like this:

- They all stand. Yes STAND – I love this!
- They give a brief (less than 15 seconds) résumé of their opinion.
- They have 30 seconds to debate a decision.
- They make a decision (or the President does!).
- They take immediate action on the decision whilst walking back to their desks.

The whole thing is done in 5 minutes. Brilliant!

Take massive **immediate** action on **every decision**

5 Take massive immediate action on every decision

Brilliant teams get things done. It's that simple. Teams break down, become ineffective, and ultimately fail because of many factors, all of which can be overcome by taking massive immediate action. When you're busy taking the correct actions, you can achieve masses. The key is immediate. Procrastination is the thin end of the wedge that removes the momentum. There are some great books on procrastination, but as I'm worried that you'll never get round to reading them, here are seven quickies to overcome team procrastination:

- **Set worthwhile goals that intensely motivate.** It's a given that if the goals motivate the team then they are more likely to take action. See Chapter 3 for more details.

- **Visualize the task as completed.** Imagine starting a team project by asking everyone to close their eyes and visualize the project completed. Seeing the outcomes exactly as they want. Then get them to link this emotionally and anchor the feeling by using the image.

- **Affirmations – do it now!** This one needs some guts but if you can get your team mates to use this simple powerful affirmation, 'Do it now', it really does get teams to take action. At the end of a brief West Wing meeting cry out, 'When are we going to do it?' 'DO IT NOW!' should be the instant response.

- **Put your team on record.** It's amazing what a little bit of visibility will do to encourage people to take action. Our project *will* be completed by the end of the month. Tell everyone – then it's a must.

- **Refuse to make excuses/rationalize.** 'Well we would have got started sooner but we had too many other things to do.' I bet you wish you had a cash bonus every time you heard those words! By refusing to make excuses, you will make your and your team's actions immediate.

- **Create a reward system for yourselves.** Will everyone get a bar of chocolate for completing phase 1 or will it be a night out on completion? Why not set up a reward fund (don't spend hours discussing it – do it or don't).

- **Overpower the biggest task first.** It feels great when you conquer a big Rock and as a team you feel unstoppable. Use the techniques in 'Brilliant rock-busting' (Chapter 6) to get this done.

Massive immediate action can be increased using lots of methods, but the best I have found come from creative use of music. Music gives immediate anchors to moments from our past (mostly positive) that help us to move into an emotional state very quickly. Take time to find some motivating music to inspire you and your team, and it doesn't have to be the over used 'Simply the Best'!

The final part of brilliant teams is knowing when and how to dismantle the team. So often teams are left to simply fall apart. Great movies have a start, middle and an end. Often the ending is the best part. Teams on the other hand have great starts, get weak in the middle and drift off in the end.

So it's worth taking a look at what you can do to end teams in a classy way. If you're working on a 90-day massive action plan I would suggest you keep the last few days for tidying. If you have recruited a 'completer finisher' (or if you are that person), get everyone to feed back to them what they have done and actions completed. Then document it. You don't need huge reports, just get it all brought together with a few notes about what happened, when and by whom. Pull together the data and ask at the final meeting the three critical questions:

1 What did we set out to achieve?

2 Did we achieve it?

3 If so, how; if not, why not?

That's it. Make the final report easy for someone in the future to pick up, use and learn from. Then you're on to a winner.

Each part of the 'Brilliant teams' chapter can be accelerated to the power of ten or more by adding one more ingredient. It is . . .

brilliant
vision

magine jumping out of bed each day with a personal vision clearly embedded in your mind. How would it feel if you were so certain of your future that you knew 100 per cent in your heart that you could achieve anything you put your mind to?

In order to create that level of certainty, your vision for brilliance must become part of your life every moment of every day. You'll do this in several ways.

The first stage is very, very simple and lots of fun. Spend some time putting together a visual representation of how it will look when you have *achieved* the goal. In the most basic form you can draw a picture (a little stick man picture would do) of you achieving brilliance in the area you want. However, with a little time and effort, you can find and cut pieces out of magazines, take photographs and or get images from the internet.

Say you have a goal that you want to visit Florida. Spend some time to get a really strong visual representation of how it would look when you have achieved the goal. You've got to get creative here. If you think, 'Wait a minute, how can I have a picture of me in Florida when I've never been to Florida?', you will quickly limit your options. Go to a travel agent, get a brochure, find a great picture, take a picture of you (with the people who you want to be there with) and stick it in the picture – you with Mickey Mouse would be great! If it isn't Mickey Mouse, get something that represents Florida for you. Whether it's going to be the coastline, the Kennedy Space Center, or Disney Land, find something that would represent it for you.

If you have a brilliance goal – for example, to be brilliant at managing a team – then create an image that sums this up for you. Would you be receiving an award? Could you get pictures of your team and have them with speech bubbles saying what a brilliant team leader you are?

What if you have a goal to be in peak physical fitness? Put your head on somebody else's body if you need to. Whatever it takes, get a great visual representation. This could take five minutes, it could take an hour, it could take a few hours, but it's a great experience to do. Then put them into a nice book – the type you would like to carry around. This image will be with you at all times.

The next stage is to write the affirmation that goes with each picture. Remember to make it personal, make it positive and put it into the present tense: the three P's. You can start by writing: I am, I have, I own or whatever it is. Go back to that holiday in Florida, you could write down, 'I am having the most amazing holiday of my lifetime in Florida now,' not, 'One day in the future I might go to Florida.' How woolly is that? How vague is that? Would Muhammad Ali have said that? No! If you want to go to Florida, then the way you're going to get there is through massive action and programming your brain to believe you are achieving it now, creating Gestalt. See a picture of you and your family and visualize them in the exact situation you wish, then write down your affirmation with passion.

If you want to be a brilliant team leader write the words: 'I am a brilliant team leader now.'

If you want to be financially free, then create an image of yourself being financially free. That may mean a zero balance on a credit card bill or a healthy bank account. Create the image then write down: 'I am financially free now.'

If you want to have incredible health, create the image and write down, 'I am in peak physical health now.' Do this with each of your goals.

The third area is to state by when you will achieve this goal. Decide on the date. Then write this date next to the goal that is to be achieved. Go through each of them and write down the date.

Brill Bit

Don't be tempted to write, 1 week, 2 months or a year's time etc. because every time you look at that goal and read that timescale it will be in the future.

A goal is just a dream without a date on it.

One of the things people tend to do is over-estimate how much we can achieve in the short term and under-estimate how much we can achieve in the long term. Be careful to get the balance right.

If you set a goal and it doesn't work out exactly how you intended it to, or if it takes a little bit longer to achieve, don't worry – it doesn't matter. The fact that you are now on the journey, the fact that you have now stepped up, that you have made a commitment towards achieving the goal is something 99 per cent of people would never do. You are on the way; that's the important thing. Enjoy the journey, go for it and make a commitment.

The next part of the process is to create this visual image and completely replace any negativity, any self-doubt that things couldn't happen and create an image in your mind with such a passion and enthusiasm that it becomes real.

The way to do this is, every morning, when you first wake up, sit and read your goals. Every night when you go to bed you sit and read your goals. Make smaller visual versions of goals and put a copy into your wallet or purse. Stick them on to your mirror so you see them several times a day. Really believe that you have achieved those goals, visualize yourself completing them, then you will to start to achieve them.

Brill Bit

Here's a cracker from my great friend Jeffrey Gitomer. He calls it 'Achieve your goals with Post-it notes'. Write down your big goals in 3–5 words. Put them on the bathroom mirror where you will see them at least twice a day. Keep looking – you will begin to act. Seeing the note there every day makes you act on it. When a goal has been completed, repost it on your bedroom mirror. Revisit your success every day while dressing!

But what if I don't achieve all my goals? I'm frightened to fail. Ever heard yourself saying that? Have you ever just not done something in case you fail? If you don't give at least one major goal a go, you won't achieve any. If you go for five and only achieve four, you're four times more successful than the ones who don't take the first step.

Brill Bit

Sometimes people say, 'I've set 10 great goals and I achieved 8 of them but not the other 2' and they beat themselves up because they didn't achieve the other two. I have a belief system which is, 'the best for all concerned will occur'. Sometimes people aren't ready to achieve a certain goal. People aren't ready to be at a certain place. Sometimes it might affect somebody else in an adverse way. So remember, the best for all concerned *will* occur. If you have the passion, the enthusiasm, the excitement for your goals, then many more are going to be achieved than fall by the wayside.

I know you will achieve them as long as you have lashings of the final ingredient – MASSIVE ACTION!

This all sounds very exciting but what about the practical actions that are needed day by day? You know, just getting up and looking at the goals and reading them is a bit like, 'no weeds, no weeds'. It's action that makes the difference.

Another great way to help with vision is to be mentally running the scenario, the outcome or the goal you want many times. This is called mental rehearsal, it's used by many different people in a variety of ways. You can sometimes see athletes mentally rehearsing on the track before they run a race, or you can see golfers mentally rehearsing before they take their swing.

By mentally rehearsing something, you are preparing your whole physiology from your brain to the tips of your toes for the activity that you're about to embark on. So, when it comes to vision, what could you mentally rehearse? Here is a list of some of the popular activities people mentally rehearse:

Communication	Other areas
Interviews	Finding a parking space
Presentations	A night out
Meetings	Golf swing
Reviews	Sporting event
A telephone conversation	Writing a letter or report
Handling a complaint	A journey
Asking for help	

I want to give you an example of how mental rehearsal works and the power of your brain. This works brilliantly with your eyes closed, so if you can, get someone to read this to you. If not, use your imagination as you read, taking breaks if you want to feel each part.

I want you to imagine that it is the hottest day of the year. It's sweltering. The temperature has been building up throughout the day and around about midday you decide to go out for a long walk. It's a really great experience as you pace along enjoying your walk.

After a few hours, you realize that your mouth is very dry, so dry that you think you have got a tongue like an old sock. The most important thing you want right now is a drink but there's nowhere around where you can get one. The only option is to walk home. As you are walking home your mouth gets drier and drier – you're desperate to get a drink.

Eventually you reach your front door. You walk into the house and no one else is in, there's only you at home. You walk into the kitchen, you think 'I must get a drink now.' You open the fridge, look inside and there is a wonderful cold bottle of mineral water, still or sparkling, your choice. Imagine you take out the bottle and open the top. You find a nice clean glass and start to pour the water into the glass.

Just before you pick up the glass you think, 'I'm going to be tidy,' so you put the bottle back into the fridge, and as you are doing so, you notice there's a lemon in the fridge. That lemon has wonderful bright yellow skin. Imagine now picking up the lemon; feel the waxiness of the skin. Wouldn't it be nice to have a little bit of lemon in that mineral water? You take a knife and slice the lemon in half. Then you take the knife again and slice a half in half again. You take the quarter of lemon, just about to drop it in the glass. But, rather than putting it into the water, imagine now you bring it to your mouth and bite into it. Imagine now biting into that lemon. How does it smell? How does it taste?

So let's have a look at what happened here. It isn't the hottest day of the year. I'm fairly sure, it might be, but the chances are it's not the hottest day of the year right now as you're reading this book. However, the more that I talked about it getting hotter and hotter and the more that I described your mouth getting drier and drier I'm sure, for most of you, your mouth did become drier. You probably started to move your tongue around; you started to move your jaw trying to get some saliva into your mouth. And then when I talked about the lemon and biting into the lemon, for most of you saliva was released into your mouth. Is it the hottest day? No! Was there a lemon? No! It was just in your imagination but you managed to get a physiological response. Your body has responded to something that you only imagined.

So by imagining something first, could we get a better physical response when we go into the true situation? Absolutely!

I heard a great story about testing mental rehearsal on a basketball team, UCLA in California. They split the team into three groups. Then they got each player to throw 100 shots and measured how many baskets each team scored. For phase two they took the three groups and gave them different types of practice. The first group was a control group; they didn't do anything different at all. The second group completed an extra hour's practice every day just throwing at the basket. That is all they would do, shoot at the basket for that extra hour every single day. The third group just mentally rehearsed for an extra hour each day, all they did was practise in their mind's eye.

They brought the three teams back together one month later. As you would expect, the control group hadn't improved but the group that had practised for one hour every single day throwing the ball had improved, in fact, they showed a good improvement. The most staggering thing of all was the group who just mentally rehearsed. All they did was one extra hour of mental rehearsal each day and their scores were greater than any of the others! This is because when they practised in their heads, the pathways of brain cells formed into an 'accurate shooting' pathway of brain cells.

Another month later, they brought the teams back together again. This time the group who had done an extra hour of physical practice every day had dropped their scores. However, the group who had just done mental rehearsal maintained their high scores.

Brill Bit

The reason the team who had been mentally rehearsing maintained high scores for longer was they had practised hitting the basket *every single time*. Every shot was successful. They never missed. So when it came to doing the exercise, they were 100 per cent sure in their minds that they could hit. Of course, not every single ball went in but they had created a pathway of brain cells that was permanent.

Start to think about the things that you could mentally rehearse and how you could get the outcomes you want.

Have you ever had to go to an important meeting where you needed to be prepared? You prepare your papers, you prepare where you're going to, you prepare transport, you get your directions, you set off in good time, but do you actually mentally prepare the meeting? With mental rehearsal you would see yourself in the meeting. You would hear the things that people were going to say. You would experience the whole feeling, the whole sensation of the meeting, before you even go through the door. Most importantly, you would see yourself being successful.

If you spent five minutes mentally rehearsing a meeting, would that meeting be more successful, less successful or exactly the same? My guess is it would be more successful. What if you were going to have a night out? Could you mentally rehearse having a great night out with friends? Of course you could. You could see yourself having a great time, meeting the right people, going to the right places, everybody getting along, having an amazing experience together.

Again ask the same question. If you spent five minutes mentally rehearsing having a great night out, would you have a better night out, a worse night out or would that night out be exactly the same? My guess is that you would have a better night out because of the experience that you have mentally rehearsed in your mind.

What about a presentation? What if you had to stand up and do a presentation in front of 500 people? Some of you are thinking, 'Oh no, I would never want to do a presentation in front of 5 people never mind 500!' But if you did, one of the great ways to prepare for a presentation is to mentally rehearse the process first. See yourself getting a standing ovation, see everybody nodding and cheerfully agreeing with what you were presenting. By doing that, do you think that you will have a better chance of making a great presentation, a worse chance or no difference? My guess is that you will have a much better chance of making a great presentation.

See yourself getting

a standing ovation.

What about in sport? If you play tennis or any other sport that requires hand-to-eye co-ordination, if you practise making shots before you actually took them, could you imagine how much better you would become? If you had to be standing in the right place on a court at the right time, if you mentally rehearse being at that right place, receiving the ball, doing great returns, would you be better? Absolutely!

Research carried out at Edinburgh University discovered that the brain processes information in much the same way in mental rehearsal as it does during actual physical activity.

So, mental rehearsal can work in many different areas of your life. Use this tool. Test it out. It is a key part of creating a vision. It's very simple yet very powerful. A few minutes invested mentally rehearsing each important area of your life will pay back many times.

You now need to start and take massive actions, practical actions that are going to make a difference. Sorry folks, brilliance is a standard and almost always equals some real hard work.

Brilliance is a **standard** and almost **always equals** some real hard work.

The first thing you are going to do is to break your goals into 90-day blocks. Take the very first goal on your list and say, 'OK, when do I intend to achieve this goal by?' It may be a 90-day goal, maybe 6 months, maybe 1 year, 5 years, 10 years. But whatever it's going to be, you need to take some action right here right now. Have a look and say, 'OK, what do I need to achieve in the next 90 days to take me closer towards reaching that goal? What do I need to have in place? What must I have done for myself? What resources do I need to have around me?' Start asking those questions. These are the key questions that make you plan.

Consider what resources you have right now and what resources you need to bring into your life towards achieving that goal. That resource could also be, 'Who do you know now who can help you?' One of the best ways to get help is by building rapport with people whom you know can help you towards achieving the goals.

The resources could be people, books, places, information, or it might be things you are going to do for yourself. Look at the different resources that need to be in place and write them down. Why are you going to write them down? I believe when you write something down, then you've made a commitment. You've made a commitment on paper, but more importantly, you have made a commitment to yourself that this is what I'm going to do. Then the key is to schedule it. By making time, writing down the commitment and clearly defining when, now it's part of a 90-day programme: it really has become a 90-day plan.

Brill Bit

Five frogs were sitting on a log. One decides to jump off; how many are left?

The answer is five. Why? Because the frog only decided to jump off. It didn't actually schedule the jump time and stick to it!

Now let's get this really started. (What do you need to achieve in the next 30 days?)

What do you **need**
to achieve in the next 30 days?

Look at your list and identify either the things that will be completed or the actions that will have happened in the next 30 days. If you are going to plan the next 30 days, why don't you plan the next 7 days? Commit to 7 days of massive action to really get the momentum started. By taking massive action for 7 days, the next 30 days are going to be easy. Take massive action for 30 days and the next 90 days are going to be even easier. Do this for 90 days and you're on a roll. Now take out your diary and schedule with as much accuracy as possible when you will take the necessary actions. You are going to achieve your goals much faster than you ever thought possible. You will be brilliant!

Most people use their diaries or calenders only to schedule meetings or events not activities. You are not most people. If you were to continue to follow this format, what would happen after the next 7 days? What about the next 24 hours? Whatever you do in the next 24 hours is going to springboard you towards what's going to happen for the next 7 days, 30 days, 90 days, 1 year, 5 years, 10 years. Yes, the next 24 hours – you cannot put things off any longer. You have made a commitment and it's time to start it now. Take some actions. Just choose 1 or 2 things that you are actually going to do. Make that call. Go and see that person. Buy and read that book. Get that resource. Talk to people. Make a commitment. Get out and take some exercise. Step up! Move towards achieving your goal. Do it right now in the next 24 hours. Schedule! Schedule! Schedule!

Finally, what are you going to do in the next 15 minutes? In the next 15 minutes you may have put down this book and that is the most critical time, because if you say, 'I enjoyed that; there were some great ideas in there and now I know them' but you are not doing them, then you have wasted your time. Because knowing something at an intellectual level, as we said right at the start, is not enough. This is about the doing. This is about taking the actions. This is about making a difference now.

In the next few pages I'm going to ask you to make a decision. Whatever decision you make, I want you to promise yourself you are going to go forwards with that decision. You are going to step up, it's going to make a difference and it's going to last, not just for 5 minutes, not for 10 minutes, 15 minutes, a week, a month, a year, it will change your life for ever – starting right here right now.

In the future, if you look back in time and you haven't taken the actions, think about what you could have missed out on by not taking action. Think about what you could have missed out on by not following through. Then say, 'This is a must, this is an absolute must now. It's not a should – it's a must that I'm going to take the actions.' Are you ready to make a decision like that?

If you are ready, you can make a commitment. Let's test that level of commitment by putting . . .

10

brilliance
into action

f I've said it once, I've said it a hundred times: Massive Action = Massive Results. Now it's time to put everything you have learned into action.

> Vision without action is a daydream. Action without vision is a nightmare. **(Japanese proverb)**

Let's pull all these ideas together and see how we can apply them to create an amazing, incredible future.

A quick recap

First of all, the *Wheel of Life* points out the areas where you must take massive action – so use the Wheel of Life on a regular basis, at least once a month. You can also plot your progress and get a balance in your life with this simple, yet effective tool.

Use the characteristics of brilliant people. Practise positive language, positive belief and positive action, in a way that engages you.

Break out of limiting beliefs, the things that hold other people back will never hold you back again. Use Pace, Team & Fun.

Think differently. Now that you understand more about how your brain works, apply those ideas and consciously send your thoughts in the right direction.

Learn how to manage stress. Use relaxation on a regular basis to help yourself get down to that alpha theta level.

Take massive action. Remember, Massive Action = Massive Results. Do it now!

You are already starting to step up. By stepping up to the areas that you think are the most important in your life, you are being brilliant. Focus on many areas for goals but a maximum of 3 for brilliance.

By understanding the basics of goal-setting using the 3 P's, you have a cause for learning and mastering the materials in this book. Remember 'I am the greatest'!

Once you decided on your areas of brilliance you said, 'OK, what am I going to do to eliminate the things that have been holding me back? What does my belief system tell me that I must eliminate?' You have started to eliminate each different part, starting with the Rock. When you get rid of that Rock, everything else becomes easier. If you have eliminated your Rock already, keep going back to your list and ask, 'What else can I eliminate now? What else can I change now? What can I focus on that's in my Circle of Influence?' Only focus on your Circle of Influence. Remember the Circle of Concern is just a pity party, where you can moan and groan all you want to but it won't change anything.

Then you looked at your values. Your values are what you build everything on. We could almost have started the book with values, because everything else comes from that. If your value system is right, if the belief system that you have alongside of your values is pushing you in the right direction, then you'll achieve all you ever need to. You now understand how to make those values easy to achieve. Who creates the rules? You create the rules. So create simple rules, rules that are going to make a big difference to you.

Have you used mental rehearsal? Before you go into a meeting, before you are having a chat with your kids, before playing a sport? By using mental rehearsal techniques, you'll see immediately and understand the difference that it makes.

Then it was time to create a personal vision. A vision with passion! You have explored what is important, where you want to go, how you are going to create visual images, and you have set a timescale for taking the necessary actions. By taking those actions, within that timescale, you've joined a tiny percentage of the population who have an understanding of how to set goals and who have actually documented their goals.

So now it's down to you. I know this stuff works. We have had thousands of people through our courses; I could show you the many letters, the many emails, or let you listen to the phone calls that we get every day from people who are telling us that these techniques make a huge difference in their lives.

That's them: what about you?

The final ingredient in the mix is to create momentum. When a rocket leaves the launch pad on a trip to the moon, it uses 95 per cent of its energy in the first 3 minutes. It's the initial push that is needed to break through. The same can be said of a pursuit of brilliance. The initial commitment, actions and removing of the limiting beliefs that hold you back are the keys to achieving brilliant results.

Take the great speakers Cicero and Demosthenes. After Cicero spoke, people would leap to their feet and talk about the great speech he had made. When Demosthenes spoke, they would jump to their feet and say, 'Let's march!' Are you going to be full of fine words or inspired by action?

You may also be thinking, 'I know a few people who need to change their ways to be brilliant before I can.' Gandhi summed it up when he said, 'Be the change you want to see in the world.' Your actions will make a bigger difference than sharing your knowledge. Though I must say I think this book would make a great gift!

Use the tools, apply them, step up and you can have a brilliant quality of life that you could only have dreamt about beforehand.

So what do you focus on if you already are, or when you become, brilliant? Easy, you'll learn . . .

11

how

to be 'Brilliant-er'–
the next level!

So what happens once you become brilliant? Is that the end?

Actually, the path towards becoming brilliant is a continuous and never-ending journey.

Being brilliant is a work in progress. However, having studied brilliant people (folk you and I would consider had already achieved brilliance) I've noticed something amazing. They just keep getting better.

Being **brilliant** is a work in progress

In this revised edition of *How to be Brilliant* I was tempted to write the 'How to be Brilliant-er' chapter as a means of giving some additional tools to those who have already achieved the highest standard but want more. But I've noticed some interesting traits in those people, they seem to have tools and techniques that keep them fresh. They don't need extra tools – they just know. Here are some of the things that I've noticed they know and do.

1 Be in competition with yourself

Once you become the very best who else is there to become better than? There's always you.

In fact, even before you become the best, if you take an opportunity to beat your old self every single day, you'll improve every single day. If that's the case, then the only way is up.

This is particularly evident in sports. Take someone like Michael Jordan who has been described as the world's greatest ever basketball player. There is no doubt that he achieved amazing successes during his career. When he was asked who his biggest competitor was, his reply was 'himself'.

Brill Bit

What do you do best (or even well) and have you become a little too comfortable? It's maybe time to be in competition with yourself and raise your game.

2 Do something totally different

Have you ever wanted to go white water rafting or visit the most incredible places on earth? What about meeting one of your heroes or taking a risk and really finding your true self?

Often we have these conversations followed by, 'Well, if I won the lottery I would . . .' The fact is you don't have to win the lottery to experience wonderful things. Most people's goals can be achieved with dedication and commitment. I think waiting for a fairy-tale lottery win is an excuse to stay inside your comfort zone rather than going for it and overcoming your fears to experience something brand new.

So what are you going to do that's completely different? I've noticed that brilliant people are very open to testing out new ideas so here's a list of 10 things to get you started:

- Run a marathon.
- Hang glide.
- Take up dancing.
- Visit a country a minimum of five hours away from home.
- Work for a charity.
- Be taught how to paint.
- Fly a plane.
- Write a book – I did!
- Take up a new sport.
- Learn a new language.

Making the decision to do something is the easy part – the challenge now is to actually go out and do it.

3 Look beyond your sector

Some people become brilliant at something **because** it is their entire focus.

Some people become brilliant at something because it is their entire focus. Then once they get to the highest level they think, 'Is this it?'

One of the real tricks in going to the next level, to be beyond brilliant and enjoy the process, is to look at other sectors, other areas, other influences. Ask yourself, 'How can I think transferable and apply those influences to my life?'

One of my mentors, David, has a brilliant technique. Whenever he travels, he visits the newsagents at the airport and stands in front of the magazine racks. Then he closes his eyes and moves his vision behind his eyelids. After a few moments he opens his eyes and, whichever magazine he looks at first, he buys.

I asked him what benefits he'd found from this. He said, 'To be honest, sometimes I find some amazing information in these magazines; other times there are only one or two things I find slightly interesting and the rest is rubbish. But I can skim pretty quickly and I can dismiss the article that won't have any use very quickly.'

He went on to tell me about an occasion he bought a copy of the *Angling Times* – a magazine for people who are obviously interested in fishing (he's not). He struggled to find an article that was interesting. But David doesn't give up and, after a short while, he did find something of interest. When he adapted it and applied it to his business, it netted him over £500,000 in one year. He also managed to find a very nice cottage in Southern Ireland which he and his family visit regularly.

There are lots of ways to look beyond your sector. Have you ever thought about doing a job swap? It may be fascinating for you to visit somebody else's place of work, for even a few hours.

Once you get into the idea of looking outside of what you already know, you will start to think about transferring ideas and applying those ideas in your life.

> **Brill Bit**
>
> The secret to looking beyond your sector is to 'think transferable'. Don't limit your thinking to the first generation of what you see. Take it two or three stages forward. You'll be amazed at what you find.

4 Find an Honest Joe '

An Honest Joe (or Honest Jo) is a person who will give you feedback on your performance in a ruthlessly honest way.

The chances are you probably won't have to look too far to find that person. It's probably someone who's close to you now and, if you were really honest with yourself, it's probably a person from whom you don't want to hear bad news. But once again it's a case of getting out of your comfort zone and listening to them. Most importantly, listen to what they say.

It can be difficult to listen carefully and not attempt to defend yourself when you are being given feedback which could be better. Here's a tip to help. When you receive this feedback think about it like 'Marks & Spencer' presents. Imagine the scene. You receive a gift on your birthday from a friend or relative and you instantly know that you don't like it, but then you notice the label. It's from M&S. Hooray, it's as good as cash. You say thank you, look at it, appreciate it then, as soon as you can, you take it back! You don't say, 'Urgh! That's horrible, what makes you think I'd wear that? Are you crazy?' (Not the best way to build rapport.) It's the same with Honest Joe feedback. Even if you disagree and won't be changing a thing, you still say, 'Thank you, I appreciate your feedback,' Bite your lip.

Brill Bit

There are lots of unofficial Honest Joes out there who are only too happy to criticise what you do. With those people it's best to 'Ignore the critics but learn from the criticism.'

Ignore the critics but learn from the criticism

My Honest Jo is my wife, Christine. As I've made a commitment to be brilliant at presenting, she watches every appearance I make and gives me feedback at the end of it. There are times when I believe I've done a brilliant job and the feedback sheets from our clients say so. However, Christine will find a quiet moment to point out the areas where I could improve, the places where I could have been more committed or where I could have listened more carefully to the questions I was asked. She'll tell me where I could have timed things a little better and how I looked and sounded. So does it work? I have recently been described as one of the top 10 professional speakers in the world and I'm still working hard to be even better.

5 Become a master re-framer

Studying brilliant people gives you the opportunity to see how they become the very best. One of the things I've noticed is that truly brilliant people who want to be even better are exceptionally good at re-framing. I don't mean replacing the wooden surround from a picture.

What I do mean is looking at situations from multiple different angles.

Here's a simple tool you can use to become a master re-framer: if you are in a situation where you have a conflict with somebody, first of all take yourself away from the conflict area, then take a moment just to close your eyes and see the situation in multiple ways.

First of all through your eyes. You'll know this view – you live it.

Then, imagine yourself elevating above the situation and take an aerial view. What do you notice about the situation now? How do you look? How do they look?

Now, move into their perspective and imagine the situation from their point of view. What can they see? What do they experience? What do they notice about the situation? How do they feel?

A few years ago I used to take one-to-one meetings with members of my team whilst sitting behind my desk. Meetings with my team were good, sometimes fantastic but rarely brilliant. I decided that if I wanted to be brilliant in this area of discussing things with my staff, then I would need to 're-frame' the meetings.

I closed my eyes and began by looking at the meeting from my perspective, then I looked using the aerial view. Finally, I looked at the view from their perspective and the first thing I noticed was that my computer screen was just slightly to the left of where they were looking. I then framed in my mind what they would be seeing when they looked at me. I was shocked. I saw myself looking at the computer screen instead of being totally focused on them.

So, I made a conscious effort from then on that every time somebody came to my office to see me, I would step out from behind my desk and meet them in a separate area.

What can you re-frame to turn a negative into a positive, to tidy up a mess or to get better?

It is no accident that the people who are the most brilliant continue to get even better but you don't have to wait until you feel you have brilliance as your benchmark before applying these skills. Do them now and you'll rapidly move closer towards your goal of being brilliant.

However it's not easy, what if doesn't all go to plan? Then you'll need to know about . . .

12

overcoming obstacles – what stops brilliance?

When *How to be Brilliant* was first published, we received many emails, telephone calls and letters from readers who have applied the tools and techniques and found that their lives are transformed. Not only did they find that they had increased wealth, health, work success, better relationships etc. but they also found brilliance in other areas of their lives too. However, we also found there was a significant group of people who, just as soon as they got started with their 'How to be Brilliant' tools and techniques, they faced setbacks.

If you don't know how to properly address these, it is very easy to stumble and fall during your first 90 days of 'massive action'. In this second edition I have focused on the top five most common setbacks and designed ways that you can overcome them to make sure that you achieve brilliance.

1 Procrastination

Even though throughout this book I suggest readers take action now and do the exercises straight away, I still find that a significant number of people read the book first and 'say' they are going to take the actions but they never do.

With this edition we have included a simple checklist to ensure you have carried out all of the exercises. You can find it on page 168. Now if you can't honestly tick each exercise as done, you can schedule in a time when it will take place.

This is very important and will really help you to become brilliant by creating momentum. When you create momentum it's much easier to keep going. Keep this action list in a highly visible place and it will stir you into action.

Brill Bit

If you want to overcome procrastination in any area keep your actions visible. If you want to take more exercise keep your training shoes next to the front door – you'll run more often! Remember – the secret isn't in the knowing – the secret is in the doing.

2 Other people

Wouldn't it be great if you were surrounded by fabulous, supportive people who really wanted you to be brilliant in all the key areas of your life and they gave you enough time, freedom and the opportunity to do everything that you've read in this book?

The reality is that some will but many won't. You will become most like the people you spend most of your time with. Think about who those people are right now. It may be that you are surrounded by very inspirational people who will stretch and encourage you. However, you may be surrounded by some people who just do not subscribe to the tools and techniques that you have been learning and actively work to prevent your progress. Then you have a very simple choice.

We have a programme for young people called 'Beyond Brilliant'. During the programme, often with teenagers, we look at who they choose to spend their time with. Sometimes it becomes blatantly obvious to these young people the reason why they are not achieving everything they want in their lives. The top reason? The people who they are spending their time with are not supportive and they are being dragged down. We then give them this piece of advice – you can either *lead your group or leave your group*.

You can either *lead your group or*
leave your group

If you choose to lead your group then you have to take on responsibilities as a leader and continue to move up to the next level, regardless of what other people think. If you don't think you can do this then maybe it's time to spend less time with the people who are holding you back.

Can you change other people? Yes, but... At the end of our presentations, one of the most common questions we are asked is: 'Well if I decide to be brilliant, what can I do about the people around me? What if they don't want to change?' I always refer them back to a wonderful quote by Gandhi: 'Be the change you want to see in the world'. In other words, stop spending time wanting to change other people and just focus on being brilliant yourself first.

Stop **spending** time wanting to change other people and just focus on being brilliant yourself first

It's amazing how quickly people see what you're doing, the difference you're making in your life. They'll quickly ask you how you're doing it.

3 Levels of energy

How would you feel if I suggested that you got out of bed an hour earlier every day and spent 60 minutes working on how to be brilliant? I guess for most people that prospect is terrifying. The chances are high that you are one of the millions of people who wake up tired every day. Low levels of energy, whether it be when you wake up, throughout the day or when you need some oomph, are one of the biggest factors that stop people from being brilliant.

There are some things you can do to increase your levels of energy very quickly so that you can be your best, feel full of energy throughout the day, work hard into the night and have the energy to get up early and feel refreshed. My guess is you'll know all five of these already but it's worthwhile reminding ourselves of them. It's also worthwhile remembering that knowing them isn't really enough it's the. . . (fill in the space!)

i) **Take exercise** – Exercise gives you energy. Not only that, it enables you to live longer, feel healthier and rejuvenate your often tired body.

ii) **Drink lots of water** – By staying hydrated, your body works better. Pure water is the number-one fuel for your body, so drink plenty.

iii) **Eat the right stuff** – I could just end this paragraph here because through the education that we've had, especially in the last few years, you know the right stuff to eat. Brilliant people are eating the right stuff every day.

iv) Look after your body before you get a health problem – Take regular massages, visit an osteopath or chiropractor and take some treatments that really look after you.

v) Create a positive attitude that supports your healthy, energetic body – By telling yourself you're tired, you have no energy or you feel ill, then you will become what you focus on. Start to tell yourself that you are the picture of health and that you have huge amounts of energy. You will find your natural energy lasting throughout the day.

4 Lack of resources

I'm always surprised when people say that they don't have the resources that they need.

Brill Bit

I once heard it said, 'It's not the lack of resources but the lack of resourcefulness that most people suffer from.'

If you really want to find the resource to do what you need to do, then you will find it. It's out there but you have to look harder, ask better questions and be more active. You have to make it a must.

The most common resource that people believe they lack is money. But this needn't be the case as we have the right attitude towards receiving money and take the right actions towards achieving it.

Simon Woodroffe, the Founder of YO! Sushi and YOtel, told me how when he needed money to start YO! Sushi he was inspired by reading Goethe. From his wisdom Simon realized an amazing truth, 'When you are truly committed the world conspires to help you in all sorts of ways you could never believe possible including the provision of financial assistance.' The part he really liked were the last few words.

If that's the case – and I believe it is – then you can create the resource that you need, be it financial, time, information, physical or mental. You just need a burning desire first, then a commitment to see it through.

5 Setbacks that are outside your control

If you believe, as I do, that everything happens for a reason then you can always look at setbacks as an opportunity to learn. Easy to write, easy to read but very challenging to do.

Sometimes you wonder 'what is the lesson?' but usually, through time and reflection, you understand that what you saw as 'setbacks' are some of the most valuable life lessons and often disguise very good reasons why a particular thing happened at a particular time.

Brill Bit

Perhaps there are forces of nature that are just looking out for us and helping us towards brilliance in our lives. Forces we can't explain.

My uncle used to say, 'If it doesn't kill you, it'll make you stronger.' As a young person I never quite knew what this meant but I think I'm starting to understand it now. The positive person I am today has grown more through dealing with the difficult times than enjoying the good times.

'Enjoy when **times are good** and accept when times are not'.

Simon Woodroffe

Your journey towards being brilliant is going to feature some setbacks, lack of time, procrastination, other people's beliefs, low energy levels and at times an apparent lack of resources. Guess what – you're no different from anybody else who has travelled on this journey before you. All you can do is take solace in the knowledge that, at the end of the day, it is worth it. Thousands of people have benefitted from *How To Be Brilliant*, and you can be inspired by some of them when you discover . . .

13

brilliance
uncovered

One of the wonderful things about creating a second edition of a book is the opportunity to share with new readers what existing readers have done. This chapter is more than testimonials: it's about reading, understanding and then applying some of the stories you read here to your own life.

Here's the key to getting the most out of this short chapter – *think transferable*. If you read the story on 'brilliant education' and don't think it applies to you because you've finished with your education days or it's not in your sector, then you'll have missed a trick. Enjoy the power of these stories, feel inspired and take action.

Think transferable.

Brilliant families – Using the Wheel of Life for family harmony

So how do you get your family to sit down, share their challenges, aspirations and spend some quality time together? That's what the Lee family in Singapore wanted and the *Wheel of Life* was the answer.

Mum had bought *How to be Brilliant* because she liked the cover (as good a reason as any) but once she started to read she became fascinated with the 'Wheel of Life' and its many applications. After completing her Wheel for the first time she decided the whole family should do theirs. She downloaded copies for everyone from my michaelheppell.com website and set herself a short-term goal to persuade her whole family (five of them) to complete their Wheels together. She changed *work* for *education* for her teenage sons and made this family event a must for everyone.

Two days later they had finished their evening meal and set about the task of completing their Wheels. Each area on the Wheel was discussed. Because Mum and Dad were open and honest it wasn't long before the whole Lee family were sharing their hopes and dreams and analyzing the Rocks that were holding them back. They were able to support and help each other work towards a balanced Wheel.

Brilliant guidance – Jane uses her advisors

Jane used to get completely overwhelmed with challenges. This heightened anxiety was something she would try to hide but the people closest to her could 'feel something wasn't right'. She decided to use the Mastermind Group idea from 'Brilliant rock-busting' to see how others would deal with the challenges she faced.

'Things that seemed hard to deal with appear simple and straightforward within my advisor's eyes,' she said. And she was right. By getting a different perspective on a challenge you often see that the problem isn't so big, or you work out a way and soon find the solution.

> By getting a different perspective on a **challenge** you often see that the problem isn't so big

Brilliant coaching

Approximately 2 out of 3 people throughout the world are now 'Life Coaches'. I'm only joking. It's really only 1 in 5, or so it feels when so many people you meet these days are either newly qualified as life coaches or they are thinking about it. I'm not a life coach, I'm a presenter, trainer and author primarily so it came as quite a surprise when I realized how many coaches were using *How to be Brilliant* as a coaching tool.

Here's how Danielle, a life coach from Norway, uses this book.

> I start with the Wheel of Life. It really helps me to understand my client and gives at least two or three areas we can work on straight away. Then I jump to 'Brilliant goal-setting' and give them that chapter as homework to read. I tell them not to read any more but human nature means they always will.

At our next meeting I ask them what they really want from life. In almost every case they have been inspired to set greater goals than if they hadn't read *How to be Brilliant*. Then I do a visualization exercise with them to give them an opportunity to feel and experience in their minds what it will be like when they achieve that goal.

I then use various tools from the book along with some of my own to plan and get focused on what they need to do. I love '90 days of Massive Action' and all of my clients work on 90-day action plans.

After the first 90 days I encourage my clients to look in detail at 'Brilliance Benchmarking'. This model is wonderful for me as it helps my clients to understand the reason why they must aim higher (to be brilliant) and why when they think they are being good they are not getting the results they want.

Brilliance in education – Freebrough College

Around 20 per cent of my work is in education. I used to joke that teachers were the hardest people on the planet to actually teach! After 10 years teaching teachers I now know it's no joke — it's true. The reality is it's never been harder for teachers. Higher expectations from parents, government and stakeholders make the actual job of teaching an ever increasing challenge. And the brilliant news is that in almost every school and college where we work these special people are rising to the challenge. And none more so than in Freebrough College.

They would be the first to admit they have some challenges, but they also have a firm belief that, no matter what is thrown at them, they'll overcome it.

They used *How to be Brilliant* at many levels. Firstly the Senior Team made a commitment to raise their benchmark to brilliance. They did this at a time when they were several months behind on a new building programme, two schools were about to be merged into one and they had gone through a very difficult inspection. This is a time when many other people would have 'put it off' until things calmed down – the fact is, in education these days, it will never calm down.

Then they involved all their staff – everyone – from Heads of Department to cleaning staff and, because they really wanted everyone to know their ambition, they arranged a separate event for local businesses and stake-holders and I was their guest speaker. They told the group with such passion about their goal to be brilliant that they got 100 per cent support and funding from several of the businesses to help finance their vision.

Then they took every pupil on a 'Brilliance into action' experience. This included 90 days of massive action campaign, which included prep-aration for exams, improving behaviour and building confidence.

The results have been incredible. As I write this I have just re-visited the school as the guest speaker at their Annual Awards Evening. Everyone I talked to had a success story, some big some small, but all brilliant.

Brilliance in a small business – From London to Leeds was all it took

When Matt, the MD of a recruitment company, saw *How to be Brilliant* in London's King's Cross Station he bought it to read on the train journey back to his office in Leeds. During that short trip, not only did he read the book (a record?) but he also made a commitment that SVB Recruitment, the firm he had started with his wife four years previously, was going to be brilliant.

Matt bought copies for all of his team and held regular West Wing meet-ings with only one agenda item, 'How to be Brilliant'. They had dozens of great ideas, from their vision 'To be recognised as the most hospitable recruitment company in the world' to their now legendary '5 o'clock Chablis' events where they invite clients to visit their office on a Friday afternoon to share their success.

Creativity shone from the team, a perfect example being in their brilliant use of language: wouldn't you love your company to have a staff recog-nition scheme where the prizes are kept in the 'rewardrobe'?

Wouldn't you love your company to have a staff **recognition** scheme where the prizes are kept in the 'rewardrobe'?

Brilliance in the public sector – Focusing on what you CAN do

One of the biggest challenges of working in a large public-sector organization is the feeling that you are a small cog in a very large machine. Sally felt that way.

'I must say, when Carole, my boss, gave me the book I was very sceptical. So it did surprise me that it was very much a book for me – I thought it was going to be about being brilliant in my job, but it was much more about being brilliant in myself – for me!

'The key moment for me came when I realized that how I felt about my work was up to me. I used the Circles of Influence versus Circles of Concern to assess what I could do to make my job more rewarding. It really worked.

'Best of all I started to reply, "Brilliant" whenever anyone asked me how I was. The look on people's faces was priceless!'

Brilliance in sport – Do you want to be in the Premiership?

Recently I have been asked to work in the wonderful world of soccer. As a person who could have been a lot better at football at school I can't help but smile as I help Premiership players to build their careers or National Teams to prepare for international duty.

One of the key messages I find top sports people take from *How to be Brilliant* is the understanding of Brilliant Belief Systems. I can't help them with their tactics or physical skills but I can help them achieve rapid change and improvement with their mental game.

So if you play a sport, ask yourself, 'What is your belief system when you go out and play?' Do you go for it and give 100 per cent all the time or do you hold back in case your going for 100 per cent causes failure? When you walk out ready for the game do you see yourself as the most feared player or do you fear the opposition?

The mental game is what takes players from fantastic to brilliant.

The **mental** game is what takes players from **fantastic** to brilliant

Brilliant relationships – A marriage rekindled using Life's Question and Values

Here's the letter just as I received it from Tony.

> Dear Michael
>
> Thank you for *How to be Brilliant* – it has saved my marriage and possibly my life. Let me tell you how so you can hopefully share this with others.
>
> I bought *How to be Brilliant* because I wanted to be better at what I spend most of my time doing now, working hard with my business partner in a new venture (two years old). The weird thing was, as I read the chapter on values I made a shattering discovery. My values and my wonderful wife's were miles apart. I almost ignored it and hoped things would 'just get better' but I couldn't get the words 'Massive Action = Massive Results' out of my head. I ran straight upstairs and shared what I discovered with my wife.
>
> Three hours later, in the early hours of the morning, we had completed the 'Life's Question' and 'Values' exercises together and for the first time I realized that I had no idea what my wife's

true values were. I know what I thought they were, I know what I thought they should be but I had no idea what they really were.

Now we are aligned and we've made some easy rules to help us to experience our core values more often. I'm more understanding, she's more tolerant and life's. . . brilliant!

Thank you

Tony

Brilliant financials – Freedom by removing my poor man's mindset

Gavin is 56 and he's spent his whole life 'just getting by'. He's never saved more than £500 in his life and, through spending everything he earns, he thought he never would.

Gavin read *How to be Brilliant* and, by the time he is 60, he will be worth a small fortune.

At first, after reading *How to be Brilliant*, Gavin did nothing. He didn't do the exercises and he didn't have a 90-day massive action plan. Six months later he was made redundant when the company where he had worked for 15 years closed. That's when he picked up *How to be Brilliant* for the second time.

This time Gavin noticed (in his words), 'I had all those characteristics you wrote about. The only thing I didn't have was a mindset that I should be doing it for me.' Gavin started his own company and, with the help of some great friends, is set to double his expected profits for the next five years. His advice? 'Don't wait until you have to do something because someone else is in control. Be yourself and you will be surprised at what you can achieve.'

Brilliant travel – See the world

Nigel was working as a sign-writer when he read *How to be Brilliant* but that wasn't where he wanted to be in his heart. He wanted to tour the world and, more than that, he wanted to share with people his excitement and passion for travel.

Within a year Nigel had reinvented himself as a travel guide. Brilliant!

But lots of people have changed jobs and are now doing the job they love because of a kick-start with *How to be Brilliant*. Craig left the world of factory flooring to become a Football Agent, Jennifer left HR to become an author and there are hundreds of others who have shared their stories with us. What I loved about Nigel was how he describes his relationship with *How to be Brilliant* now, 'I use it like a tool bag in the form of a diary. It gives me that help when my direction gets a little lost.'

I could write another book based on the successes of people who have used *How to be Brilliant* but at the end of the day this book was written for one person only and that's you.

I hope I have challenged you to have brilliance as your benchmark and to start with 90 days of massive action. Now that you know it – the secret is to do it. So go on, be brilliant!

Brilliant leverage

When Jayne confessed to being a hoarder and having a house full of junk which she could 'never get round to throwing out', it took the guts of the trainer on her time management programme to come up with a brilliant solution. He asked for her address, asked how many bags of junk and rubbish she thought she could fill, and in front of the rest of the group called the local authority and arranged for 40 bags of rubbish to be collected 3 weeks later. Jayne got over the initial shock and suddenly realized that it was time to take action. Within 1 week she had filled the 40 bags and went on to fill a further 20 with rubbish and a further 30 for charity shops! 90 bags of junk had filled her life. It's amazing what you'll do for a man in a van!

How to be brilliant exercise checklist

How have you done? Take a look at the list below and ask yourself, 'As I read this book did I do it or do I just know it?' Remember: *the secret isn't in the knowing it's in the doing.*

So ensure you have completed and ticked off all of the tasks below and you'll be well on the road to brilliance!

✔

1   Completed your Wheel of Life.   ☐

2   Started the bonus 30-day challenge to change your language.   ☐

3   Began conversations with 5 strangers in 24 hours.   ☐

4   Learned to relax.   ☐

5   Written long-term goals: 90 days; 1, 5 and 10 years using the 3 P's.   ☐

6   Created your written commitment to being brilliant.   ☐

7   Listed everything that holds you back and identified 'the Rock'.   ☐

8   Re-framed your language based around your Rock.   ☐

9   Completed Circles of Influence versus Circles of Concern.   ☐

10   Found a mentor.   ☐

11   Created a Mastermind Group.   ☐

12   Identified your Life's Question.   ☐

13   Rewritten your Life's Question.   ☐

14   Identified your current values and put them in order.   ☐

15   Written down the description of the person you ultimately want to become.   ☐

16 Rewritten your values and put them in order. ☐

17 Created the rules for your new values and created a visual
image of them. ☐

18 Written your Brilliant Vision Checklist:

   i)   Selected visual images. ☐
   ii) Created a vision book. ☐
   iii) Written the 3 P's affirmations. ☐
   iv) Noted dates they will be achieved. ☐
   v)   Created a list of resources and people who can help. ☐
   vi) Written 30-, 7- and 1-day massive action plans. ☐

19 Registered with www.michaelheppell.com and asked for
the free bonus chapter. ☐

Appendix

Michael Heppell Ltd company values

Brilliance

We are brilliant in all our actions, we 'step up' and go the extra mile towards achieving our goals.

Integrity

We tell the truth and focus on delivering correct information and feedback to each other and our clients.

Positive belief

We use positive language, tackle challenges in a positive way and choose to see a positive side of every given situation. We understand that we create our own belief systems based on the evidence we search for, so we choose to create positive empowering belief systems.

Shared goals

We share our goals with each other and make a commitment to help each other achieve those goals. We understand that by sharing goals we do so in confidence.

2nd mile and surprise

We continuously go the 2nd mile and surpass our clients' expectations. We, when appropriate, create pleasant surprises for our clients.

Family first

We believe that our families will come first. This means that it is expected we support our families and communicate when we are doing this to our colleagues and, if necessary, clients.

Fun!

We create a genuine, fun atmosphere in our work and we create a place where we can express ourselves in creative and supportive surroundings. We give our clients fun experiences. We ensure our fun experiences are not at the expense of others.

Best value

We provide best value for our clients and if requested give detailed break-downs of any costs incurred. We expect best value from our suppliers and business partners and search for this when we engage them with our company.

Team respect and communication

We respect each other and work together for a common goal. We communicate respectfully to one another. We do what we say we will do. We turn up on time and work until the job is done. We communicate with each other when challenges arise and seek first to understand.

Learning

We are committed to lifelong learning and actively encourage an environment where learning can take place.

Free Stuff, Seminars, Presentations, Training Programmes and Events

Would you like to come on a Michael Heppell programme or have Michael speak at your next event, motivate your team or get you or your business on track? To find out more contact the Michael Heppell Team.

Visit www.michaelheppell.com

Hadrian Business Centre
Church Street
Haydon Bridge
Hexham
Northumberland
NE47 6JG

Telephone 0845 67 33 336
Fax 01434 688666

International +44 1434 688555

Email: info@michaelheppell.com

To be added to our free online newsletter service simply visit www.michaelheppell.com and sign up. Tell us that you have read *How to be Brilliant* and we'll send you a free bonus chapter and a complimentary audio programme called '50 Brilliant Free Things'.

Thank you to. . .

Bill & Liz Heppell for Brilliant parenting
Andrew Heppell for Brilliant big brothering
Lea McConnell for being a Brilliant best school friend
Gav, Nonk, Sav, Cookie, Sev, Nessy & Carolyn for Brilliant teens
Tommy & Nora Cartmell for a Brilliant love of youth
Rev Barrie Lees for Brilliant guidance
Uncle Donald, Aunty Elaine & family for Brilliant Summers
Aunty Ethel and Uncle Alan for a brilliant Sunday School
The Officers & volunteers of the Boys' Brigade for Brilliant youth work
Jimmy Severs for being ruddy Brilliant
Kevin O'Neil for Brilliant Teaching
Janice Smith for Brilliant big teas
Paul Raisbeck for being a Brilliant roadie, still
Lisa Raisbeck for Brilliant rabbit feeding
Edgar & Nug for a Brilliant band
All my colleagues for Brilliant work times
Allan Percival for seeing Brilliance
Newcastle Magic Circle for Brilliant dexterity
Gary Smith for Brilliant events
Colin Gregg for Brilliant fundraising
Darren Sowerby for Brilliant technology
David Grant for Brilliant belief
Claire Hayhurst the Brilliant Iron woman
Sir Paul Nicholson for Brilliant vision
David Brown for a Brilliant challenge
Belinda Jayne Sloan for the Brilliant Common Purpose
Prof. John MacBeath for the most Brilliant mind
Richard Watts for Brilliant trimming
Jack & Norma Black for a Brilliant life lesson
Cliff Walker for a Brilliant opportunity
Steve & Yvette Mitchell for Brilliant fun in the sun
Ian Smith for Brilliant team building
Justine Hayhurst for Brilliantly being there
Chris Hampton for Brilliant fast fun
Jill Telfer for Brilliant Godmothering
Jo Walker for Brilliant fingers

Dr Fiona Ellis for Brilliant Osteopathy
Ray Cranston for Brilliant 'slippa's'
Jeffrey Gitomer for Brilliant sales training
James Pink for Brilliant humour
Wil Cheung for Brilliant hospitality
Martin Warden & Hi Lights for Brilliant Sound & Light
All at the Design Group Newcastle for Brilliant creativity
David Miller for Brilliant bacon & stilton baps and total faith
David Bell for a Brilliant introduction
Dave Thorp for Brilliant film making
Peter Smithson and HSBC for Brilliant banking
The Lamb family for being Brilliant neighbours
Robert Savage for Brilliant Bondi experiences
Stephen Deakin for Brilliant Five-Star service
Mo Hanslod for Brilliant persistence
The locals at the Hadrian in Wall for Brilliant nights out
Doreen Soulsby for being a Brilliant first Personal Assistant
Colin Kendall for truly Brilliant production
Nicola Cook for Brilliant enthusiasm
Ravinder Cheema for a Brilliant first impression
Laura Scott for Brilliant care
Jeremy Taylor for Brilliant chairmanship with friendship
Anton & Margi for Brilliant friendship
Stevie Pattison-Dick for Brilliantly telling everyone
Joan & Martin Fisher for Brilliantly being 'our kid'
Alan Wareham for Brilliantly demystifying the web
Ann & Mike Burch for Brilliant birthdays
Jesmond Dene House – a Brilliant venue
Dawson & Sanderson for Brilliant travel
Peter Field the Brilliant coach
Glyn Davies the Brilliant student
Sarah Scott for Brilliantly diving in to help
Irene Dorner for Brilliantly showing how business and friendship really works
Simon Woodroffe for being BrilliYOnt
Vanessa Thompson for Brilliantly being the world's greatest PA
Matt and Davina Robertson for Brilliantly 'sharing the love'
Taxi Mark for Brilliant driving

The Michael Heppell staff; past, present and future for making it 'a
Brilliant day'
Sam Jackson for a Brilliant revision
Everyone at Pearson for Brilliant Publishing
Rachael Stock for Brilliant editing
You for Brilliantly reading this far

& to everyone else who has touched my life, you know who you are,
thank you for Being Brilliant

and God for every Brilliant thing

Inside cover photography by Susan Bradley

Cartoons by Steve Burke at The Design Group, Newcastle upon Tyne